YORK NOTES

Animal Farm

George Orwell

Notes by Wanda Opalinska

Longman   York Press

YORK PRESS
322 Old Brompton Road, London SW5 9JH

ADDISON WESLEY LONGMAN LIMITED
Edinburgh Gate, Harlow,
Essex CM20 2JE, United Kingdom
Associated companies, branches and representatives throughout the world

First published 1997

ISBN 0-582-31329-5

Designed by Vicki Pacey, Trojan Horse
Illustrated by Steven Player, Artists Partners
Phototypeset by Gem Graphics, Trenance, Mawgan Porth, Cornwall
Produced by Longman Asia Limited, Hong Kong

CANCELLED

CONTENTS

PREFACE

York Notes are designed to give you a broader perspective on works of literature studied at GCSE and equivalent levels. We have carried out extensive research into the needs of the modern literature student prior to publishing this new edition. Our research showed that no existing series fully met students' requirements. Rather than present a single authoritative approach, we have provided alternative viewpoints, empowering students to reach their own interpretations of the text. York Notes provide a close examination of the work and include biographical and historical background, summaries, glossaries, analyses of characters, themes, structure and language, cultural connections and literary terms.

If you look at the Contents page you will see the structure for the series. However, there's no need to read from the beginning to the end as you would with a novel, play, poem or short story. Use the Notes in a way that suits you. Our aim is to help you with your understanding of the work, not to dictate how you should learn.

York Notes are written by English teachers and examiners, with an expert knowledge of the subject. They show you how to succeed in coursework and examination assignments, guiding you through the text and offering practical advice. Questions and comments will extend, test and reinforce your knowledge. Attractive colour design and illustrations improve clarity and understanding, making these Notes easy to use and handy for quick reference.

York Notes are ideal for:
- Essay writing
- Exam preparation
- Class discussion

Wanda Opalinska (M.A.) is a teacher of English and History and an Assistant Examiner for a major examining board. She now teaches in Croydon and would like to thank Alex Wordsworth and pupils at both St. Thomas More, Chelsea and Whitgift School, Croydon for their involvement with this project.

The test used in these Notes is the Longman edition, 1991, edited by Trevor Millum.

Health Warning: This study guide will enhance your understanding, but should not replace the reading of the original text and/or study in class.

PART ONE

INTRODUCTION

HOW TO STUDY A NOVEL

You have bought this book because you wanted to study a novel on your own. This may supplement classwork.

- You will need to read the novel several times. Start by reading it quickly for pleasure, then read it slowly and carefully. Further readings will generate new ideas and help you to memorise the details of the story.
- Make careful notes on themes, plot and characters of the novel. The plot will change some of the characters. Who changes?
- The novel may not present events chronologically. Does the novel you are reading begin at the beginning of the story or does it contain flashbacks and a muddled time sequence? Can you think why?
- How is the story told? Is it narrated by one of the characters or by an all-seeing ('omniscient') narrator?
- Does the same person tell the story all the way through? Or do we see the events through the minds and feelings of a number of different people.
- Which characters does the narrator like? Which characters do you like or dislike? Do your sympathies change during the course of the book? Why? When?
- Any piece of writing (including your notes and essays) is the result of thousands of choices. No book had to be written in just one way: the author could have chosen other words, other phrases, other characters, other events. How could the author of your novel have written the story differently? If events were recounted by a minor character how would this change the novel?

Studying on your own requires self-discipline and a carefully thought-out work plan in order to be effective. Good luck.

Early life

The novelist and journalist Eric Arthur Blair – or George Orwell as he was better known – was born in Bengal, India on 25 June 1903. His father was an official in the Indian Civil Service and Eric returned with his mother and two sisters to England.

Throughout his childhood he felt a sense of isolation and, on his return to Britain, was deeply aware of his family's relative poverty, factors which were to influence his later writing.

Education

At the age of eight, Orwell entered St Cyprian's, a prep school which he would criticise in his work. He later gained a scholarship to Eton which he attended between 1917 and 1921. Although Orwell himself denied that his experiences at Eton had any lasting effect on him, he later praised its humanity and tolerance of individualism.

Orwell had a conventional childhood as a member of the upper-middle class. His subsequent decision to join the Indian Imperial Police in 1922 rather than take the conventional path to Oxford or Cambridge shows that he was prepared to think and do things differently to others. He resigned from his post five years later, unhappy about the way in which the British ruled India.

Later life

Some commentators have suggested that the disgust and guilt he felt whilst in the police influenced his decision in 1927 to go to Paris and take a series of poorly-paid and menial jobs. This resulted in his first book, *Down and Out in Paris and London* (1933). Certainly, a concern for those worst off in society is apparent from his earliest work.

Orwell's politics are fascinating in that although a socialist writer he became progressively more anti-Communist and was also patriotic. When the Second

World War broke out, he tried to enlist, only to be rejected on the grounds of ill-health. He then joined the Home Guard and worked for the BBC's Indian Service, broadcasting to Malaysia.

His journalistic output steadily increased. In 1943–5 he was the literary editor of the *Tribune*, having contributed several articles to the *Observer* and *Manchester Evening News*. His first wife Eileen died in 1945 and he married Sonia Brownell in 1949. In 1947 he moved to the Scottish Hebridean island of Jura with his adopted son and his sister. His health worsened and in 1949 he was moved to a sanatorium in Gloucestershire. In 1950, a few days before he was to visit Switzerland in the hope of improving his health, he died of tuberculosis.

Novels

It was in the late twenties that Blair took the pseudonym (see Literary Terms) George Orwell. Several people have commented on the significance of his pen-name which combines the name of the patron saint of England and a river he knew well in Suffolk – suggesting that the name was chosen for patriotic reasons.

His other novels are:
- *Burmese Days* (1934)
- *A Clergyman's Daughter* (1935)
- *Keep the Aspidistra Flying* (1936)
- *The Road to Wigan Pier* (1937)
- *A Homage to Catalonia* (1938)

His first popular success *Animal Farm* was published in 1945. This work was a satire (see Literary Terms) on political tyranny and its effects on the individual, a theme which was developed in his later novel *1984* which was published in 1949.

Farm life   As the title suggests, the novel is set on a farm. Orwell goes to some length to create a realistic depiction of life on a farm. The minutiae of farm life, the trips to the market, the feeding and watering and indeed milking of animals are all described. The animals are anthropomorphic (see Literary Terms), although they still behave in ways characteristic of their species.

Fairy story   The work is subtitled 'a fairy story', drawing readers' attention to the artificial nature of what is about to unfold. *Animal Farm* appears to be a book which describes in simple language the events of life on a particular farm. However, it is not really a fairy story – it doesn't have a happy ending.

The novel is closer to another genre – that of the fable (see Literary Terms). These works (such as *Aesop's Fables*) utilise animal characters to make serious moral points. Characters do not behave in a naturalistic or realistic way but are symbolic of certain attitudes or viewpoints. Animals are especially suited to this – which is one reason why they are often the main characters in children's books (such as *Wind in the Willows* or the *Deptford Mice Trilogy*). They do not have to be as 'realistic' as characters in other novels.

Orwell made it clear in his Preface to the original edition of the text that he had a purpose in writing the book. It was a veiled criticism of the regime in the Soviet Union, a regime that at the time of writing was an ally of Britain's. At this time, it was difficult in Britain to criticise Russia. Orwell's book was rejected several times. Calling the novel a fairy story was one way to obscure his real purpose in writing the book and it also suggested that the events portrayed were simply fanciful rather than based in fact.

The apparently innocent form of *Animal Farm* hides its true content. The use of a simple storyline and straightforward characters meant that Orwell's comments on his subject could be transmitted to the widest audience in its most readable form.

A satire

You may have read another famous satire, Gulliver's Travels *by Jonathan Swift.*

Animal Farm has also been described as a satire (see Literary Terms) on political power. A satire is a piece of writing that attacks a person or idea making it look ridiculous or unpleasant. Ironic humour (see Literary Terms) is often used to draw the reader's attention to the follies that the author is attacking.

- *Animal Farm* is satirical in its selection of animals to represent different historical figures or ideas. These are generally negative representations. The public are seen as sheep, the revolution's leaders as pigs, for example.

Look at the comment on the cat's behaviour when voting, on page 6.

- The novel is a warning about the ways in which power can be abused by individuals. Orwell achieves this by showing the reader that the characters' opinions and actions are ridiculous in terms of what they do or say (as in Chapter 9, when Napoleon orders 'Spontaneous Demonstrations'. Can something spontaneous be ordered?). The narrator's comments and the style of writing can also do this.
- A satire is effective as the author expects the reader to be aware of the way in which the characters should behave. This is made clear by Major's speech in Chapter 1 which sets out a standard of correct behaviour which, as we see as the novel progresses, the pigs do not follow.

An allegory

Elsewhere Orwell described the book as an allegory (see Literary Terms).

- The period in which the action takes place is not specified but it appears to be that of the 1940s (when the book was written).
- The book deals essentially with the events of the Russian Revolution.

Tsar's rule

Under Tsar Nicholas II, the Russian ruling class lived in luxury in comparison to the rest of the population. Peasants lived in appalling conditions. Food shortages were common.

- In February 1917, increased agitation and rebellion resulted in the February Revolution and the removal the Tsar from the throne.
- The Provisional Government was overthrown in October 1917 by the Communist Party (Bolsheviks) led by Lenin. They seized the Winter Palace.

The Communists in power

Lenin took many of his ideas from Karl Marx, in particular from his work *Das Kapital* which proposed a society based on equality and freedom. One of the tools used by the Bolsheviks to spread their revolution was the use of simple slogans.

From 1918–1921 there was civil war. Foreign countries were alarmed at the idea that Communism would spread quickly and so sent troops to defeat them. The Communists eventually won, gaining tenuous control over the Soviet Union.

The struggle for power

In 1924, Lenin died. A struggle for power between Trotsky and Stalin followed. Trotsky had been the strategist behind the Red Army's success in the Civil War and was seen as a brilliant speaker. He believed that for the Soviet Union to be safe, the revolution had to be spread throughout the world in a 'Permanent Revolution'. Stalin was far more reticent and had built up a network of support through his patronage of other posts and presented himself as a moderate. In opposition to Trotsky, he felt that the country's security lay in building up her defences, 'Socialism in one Country'. Stalin worked hard to undermine Trotsky and in 1927, the latter was forced to leave the Soviet Union and, in 1929, he was sentenced to permanent exile. Stalin continually blamed him for any problems the country suffered. He was said to be working with the Soviet Union's enemies to overthrow the government.

The Soviet Union under Stalin

By 1928, Stalin dominated the government, building up a cult of personality. His rule seemed to have little in common with the ideas proposed by either Lenin or Marx. In addition, his own views and policies seemed inconsistent. In 1921 he had opposed Trotsky's plans to industrialise the country – only to do exactly that (with the Five Year Plans) when Trotsky was exiled. These Five Year Plans were extremely unpopular and set unrealistically high targets of production. Another policy to collectivise the farms met with equally strong opposition especially with the kulaks (see Political Terms). Many burned their land and killed their animals rather than let the government take them. However, by the end of the 1930s the Soviet Union emerged as a major industrial power – but the cost in terms of human suffering was huge. In addition, Stalin frequently reinvented his history and that of the Soviet people. Past enemies were presented to the people as allies and vice versa. Propaganda was a frequently used tool which further emphasised the control Stalin had on Soviet life.

Any opposition to Stalin in these years was ruthlessly and brutally crushed. Those who were thought to oppose him were exiled or executed. In many cases 'show trials' were staged in which people confessed to 'crimes' that they had not committed. These purges decimated Soviet society and created a climate of fear.

Stalin felt that the communist state was isolated and at risk from other powers. The Soviet Union joined the League of Nations in 1934 and tried to join an alliance against Hitler. This was unsuccessful and Stalin then signed a treaty with the German leader in 1939. The Nazi-Soviet pact gave the Soviet Union a chance to build up her defences, even though it seemed to go against all that Lenin and Trotsky had said. In 1941, the Germans invaded and the Russian people again suffered terribly. Stalin, Roosevelt and Churchill met at the Tehran conference in 1943. It seemed that the Soviet Union, America and Britain were now allies.

Direct parallels

Certain real historical events correspond directly with events in the novel. The events in the book do not follow Soviet history exactly but the following are the main points of comparison:

- Communism was strongly influenced by the ideas of Karl Marx who believed that life could be explained in economic and social terms. The rich capitalist class exploited the lower proletariat (see Political Terms) and this situation could only be reversed by revolution. Many of Marx's ideas lie behind Major's speech in Chapter 1.
- The Communist Party under the leadership of Lenin rose and took power, seizing control of the empire and executing the Romanovs (the Tsar's family), as the animals revolted against Jones.
- After the Revolution, Trotsky and Lenin established a communist society in the Soviet Union (as it was now called). All property, wealth and work was meant to be divided equally between all individuals. The pigs attempt to create a similar society after they defeat Jones and change the farm's name to *Animal Farm*.
- Forces loyal to the Tsar, helped by countries abroad who did not want communism to spread throughout Europe, invaded Russia. In the same way, Jones and his men attempt to recapture the farm in Chapter 4.
- However, after Lenin's death a struggle for power took place between Trotsky and Stalin. Trotsky, although favoured by Lenin, was ousted by Stalin who tried to remove all trace of him – even removing Trotsky's image from certain photographs. Napoleon and Snowball disagree on virtually every issue. At a

meeting in the barn, Napoleon drives Snowball from the farm. Snowball is later depicted by Napoleon and Squealer as an enemy of 'Animalism' and his contribution to the 'Battle of the Cowshed' is distorted.

Look at the location of these events in the novel.

- The Soviet union endured several famines as the result of Stalin's economic policies. The animals suffer increasingly from hunger after Napoleon comes to power.
- Stalin's power increased so that he had complete control over the Soviet Union. Napoleon uses a similar combination of terror and propaganda to become dictator.
- Stalin insisted that all farms should come under state control (i.e. be collectivised). He also tried to modernise Soviet industry, symbolised in the novel by the windmill. Napoleon instructs the hens to sell their eggs, but they smash them rather then let him sell them, in the same way that the peasants opposed collectivisation.

Napoleon's rise to power clearly mirrors that of Stalin. They are both seen as ruthless tyrants.

- Anyone who was a threat to Stalin was executed or sentenced to hard labour in Siberia, often following a 'show trial' in the same way that Napoleon executes the 'traitors' in Chapter 7.
- In an effort to protect the Soviet Union from attack, Stalin negotiated with both Britain and Germany. His treaty with Germany was seen as worthless when Germany invaded the Soviet Union in 1941. This mirrors Napoleon's dealings with Frederick and Snowball and Frederick's duplicity in paying for the timber in forged notes.
- At the Tehran conference in 1943, the Soviet Union, Britain and the United States of America presented themselves as allies. Within a few years, the Cold War had begun which placed the Soviet Union against the West. The pigs and men have dinner together but their friendship is destroyed when both sides are discovered to have cheated at cards.

PART TWO

SUMMARIES

GENERAL SUMMARY

Chapters 1–2:
Manor Farm –
a dream of the
future

The drunken farmer, Mr Jones, is trying to put the farm to bed. He is unable to do this properly. In contrast, Major – a boar who is respected by the animals – calls a meeting in the barn, so the other animals can listen to his dream about life on a farm without the cruelty and suffering inflicted upon them by mankind. A few days later, Major dies but his ideas continue to preoccupy the animals.

Jones and his men, drunk again, neglect their duties and the animals decide to revolt. Napoleon and Snowball (two young boars) take charge.

In keeping with Major's instructions, basic rules are established and the need for equality and freedom is stressed. These rules, now termed 'Animalism,' are painted onto the wall for all to see. However, few of them can read them. The pigs soon become literate and Snowball institutes classes for the others. Their new way of life is more efficient and happier than before. Their harvest is much larger and no animal tries to cheat another – they appear to have created a perfect society.

Chapters 3–4:
After the
revolution

A few problems are noticed however: the cow's milk disappears and the windfall apples vanish. Both, it is later made clear, have been taken by the pigs. One of them, Squealer, tells the animals that this is necessary to maintain the health of the leaders.

Chapters 5–6:
The struggle
for power

Gradually a rift between Napoleon and Snowball becomes apparent. This comes to a head over the idea to build a windmill. Napoleon sets his dogs on Snowball who is forced to flee the farm. Napoleon then curtails several more of the animals' rights. Four porkers protest against this but are silenced by the dogs.

Napoleon then tells the animals that the plans for the windmill will go ahead. The animals are surprised but say nothing. Winter comes and the animals' lives are hard. They are constantly working to build the windmill but progress is slow.

The animals are told that Napoleon has started to trade with other farms. This confuses the animals, who are persuaded by Squealer that Major did not forbid this. The pigs then move into the farmhouse and break the Fourth Commandment by sleeping in beds. This also is explained away by Squealer as necessary for the defence of the farm. An alteration to the Commandment is painted onto the wall.

A gale destroys the windmill just as it has been completed. Napoleon declares that it is an act of sabotage by Snowball and pronounces the death sentence upon him. Life for the animals continues to be hard as they attempt to rebuild the windmill.

Chapters 7–9: Napoleon and the reign of terror. Other farms begin to hear rumours that the animals on Animal Farm are starving. To prevent such gossip spreading, Napoleon takes the farm agent Whymper on a tour of the farm, showing him full bins of food. Mr Whymper does not know that the bins have been filled with sand and a thin covering of food lain on top of them. Napoleon decides to sell some timber. He is unsure whether to sell it to Pilkington or Frederick. When he thinks he should deal with Frederick, the animals are told that Snowball is hiding on Pilkington's farm and vice versa.

Four porkers are executed in front of the other animals along with three hens who also defied Napoleon over his demand that they sell their eggs. The other animals are horrified by what they have seen. They begin to sing 'Beasts of England' but are told by Squealer that this song is now banned.

Napoleon finally sells the timber to Frederick whose money turns out to be forged. Napoleon declares the death sentence on Frederick. Frederick then invades the farm and destroys the windmill. The 'Battle of the Windmill' is declared a victory. The pigs find a crate of whisky and drink it.

The winter brings even greater suffering to the animals. Food is very scarce and the cart-horse (Boxer) collapses and is driven from the farm in a van that belongs to a knacker. The other animals try to warn Boxer but he is too weak to escape and is driven off to his death. The pigs then buy another crate of whisky and celebrate his death. The next morning a further alteration is found to the Commandments on the barn wall.

Chapter 10:
The dream
betrayed

Years have passed and most of the animals that originally fought for the revolution are now dead. The younger animals do not understand the ideals that the animals originally fought for. The windmill has been rebuilt and plans are under way for a further one but the animals' life is no more comfortable than before.

The pigs and dogs now run the farm for Napoleon who has complete control over the other animals. Clover (a cart-horse) is horrified to see Squealer walking on his hind legs and alerts the other animals. A long line of pigs emerge from the house, with Napoleon at their head. They carry whips.

The Commandments have been removed from the wall. In their place is one slogan. It reads 'All Animals are Equal But Some Animals Are More Equal Than Others'. The rest of Major's rules are broken rapidly.

The pigs wear clothes, smoke and read newspapers. They even invite the humans to dinner.

The novel ends with the farm animals watching the humans and pigs at dinner together, although an argument breaks out when Pilkington and Napoleon cheat at cards.

DETAILED SUMMARIES

CHAPTER 1

Both Mr and Mrs Jones are seen from the start of the book as unattractive characters. List the activities in which they are seen to indulge.

The owner of Manor Farm, Mr Jones (who has had too much to drink), tries to finish his chores before he goes to bed. The hens' coop is left open and once the farmer has gone into the house the animals are able to gather for Major's meeting in the barn. At the meeting, Major tells the animals about his dream and encourages them to think of a vision of the future in which they will be able to govern themselves and live in freedom and peace. Major bequeaths a set of rules for the animals to live by to avoid becoming like their enemy, man. They are never to walk on two legs or to live in a house.

Major teaches them the song the 'Beasts of England', the words of which he has remembered from his dream. The animals' singing wakes Jones, who fires his gun into the animals in an effort to suppress the noise. The animals flee to their beds.

MANOR FARM – A DREAM OF THE FUTURE

COMMENT   There is little indication as to what the story is going to
be about at the start. The reader is involved through the
convincing description of farm life.

The pigs are seen as natural leaders from the start.
Major himself is a pig and the other pigs make their
way to the front as though that is their natural position.
It is interesting to note that Major describes his life as
being one of luxury, suggesting that life for the pigs is
comparatively easy. Major is established by Orwell as
being superior to the humans. Jones is seen as unfit to
manage the farm whereas Major is 'highly respected'
(p. 1) by the other animals.

*Reread the
description of the
animals as they
enter the barn.
Note the qualities
each animal
possesses.*

Orwell uses the scene in the barn to introduce the
animals and their characters to the reader. The animals
are anthropomorphic (see Literary Terms) but still
retain enough animal characteristics for them to be
credible as farm animals; they behave in ways
appropriate to their species.

The animals' behaviour on the straw gives the reader
clues as to their behaviour in the novel and their
characters are established in a way that they can develop
in line with the story. Boxer and Clover are shown
'walking very slowly and setting down their vast hairy
hoofs with great care lest there should be some small
animal concealed in the straw' (p. 2). The description of
the animals' attributes is important for later events in
the story (see Characters). The reader is encouraged to
feel sympathetic towards the animals from the start.
This is crucial to the novel's success.

Major's speech   Major states that the life of the animals on the farm is
one of 'misery and slavery' (p. 3). This is not through
the poverty of the land but because the animals are
exploited by man, their only enemy. He 'consumes
without producing' (p. 4) and fails to reward them for
the produce that he takes. Major's speech is closely

based on the beliefs of Karl Marx, a German philosopher (see Themes). Humans in the pig's speech take the place of the capitalists in Marxist thinking. In the same way, the farm animals serve as the proletariat (see Political Terms) in the book. The capitalists exploit them by working them hard in return for minimal pay. The workers are therefore not allowed to enjoy the result of their own labour. Marx believed that this would only be solved by a revolution of the workers in an armed uprising against the capitalists.

The reader's sympathies are engaged by Major's cataloguing of the animals' sufferings under man. Man exploits the animals and takes their produce from them, giving them the bare minimum in return. This suffering and cruelty is seen as universal. Further sympathy is elicited from the reader when Major states that he knows that he is dying (p. 3). According to Major 'No animal in England is free' (p. 3). The only solution is to rebel against man. If man is the only enemy then the animals must be united against him. There should be 'perfect unity' as 'All animals are comrades' (p. 5). They should thus never resemble man in any way or imitate him. Major's proposed new society is based on equality as 'All animals are equal' (p. 6).

Is it unrealistic to expect behaviour to change?

The element of realism in the novel is introduced directly after Major's speech when the dogs attack the rats. Such actions directly contradict what Major has just said. The rats represent the majority of the rural peasants whom the revolutionaries tried to shape to their way of thinking. They are not natural allies of the workers. By including this scene Orwell seems to suggest that human behaviour is essentially selfish and ruthless.

Major's speech also serves as a benchmark by which to judge the pigs' subsequent actions. He establishes and

Discuss how far you think the use of violence is justified in achieving one's aims.

predicts many events which will become true – such as Boxer's eventual fate. The irony (see Literary Terms) is that this occurs under the pigs' tyranny, not man's. Major presents the view that the only solution to Jones's tyranny is to revolt. This suggests that he endorses the idea of an armed struggle, which he sees one day as inevitable.

There are indications that the promised utopia will never materialise. The animals' society is not an equal one – three pigs are seen as pre-eminent from the first page of the novel; taking pride of place in the barn. Some animals are protective to others, whilst others seem intent on fighting amongst themselves. Some sections of the community, like the cat, are simply not to be trusted. The irony of the first chapter is clear in that it establishes through Major's speech an idealised vision of the future in contrast to the suffering under Jones. The eventual progress of Animal Farm shows that as the pigs turn Major's ideas on their head, they distortand corrupt the principles of Animalism. The animals' faith in their leaders is systematically betrayed by the pigs.

GLOSSARY   **Willingdon Beauty** a pedigree name

confinements pregnancy, in which they are 'confined' or kept away from other animals

'Clementine', 'La Cucuracha' popular songs of the 1930s and 1940s

CHAPTER *2*

Look at the descriptions of Snowball and Napoleon. Consider how this prepares you for later events.

The second chapter opens with Major's death. The pigs are inspired by his dream and plan for revolution. Three pigs in particular are pre-eminent in this: Snowball, Napoleon and Squealer. They form a philosophy or system of beliefs from Major's instructions which they term 'Animalism'.

Jones, neglectful as ever, forgets to feed or milk the

animals. They rebel against him, driving him and his men out. The animals are amazed at what they have achieved and destroy all reminders of Jones's control over them and the instruments he used to punish and control them. The revolution they had hoped for has come about sooner than they expected. The fact that all the animals are not equally delighted at the sequence of events is illustrated by Mollie's desire to continue wearing ribbons.

Napoleon immediately gains control of the food supply – why is this a shrewd move?

The pigs begin to spread their creed amongst the animals. Literacy classes are given and the most important of Major's guidelines (now reduced and simplified into the Seven Commandments) are written on the wall of the barn for the other animals to read and learn and to keep before them as an example of how to live. The animals then begin the harvest and start to work for their future. The cows are milked and the hens look forward to having the milk placed into their mash. However, upon the animals return from work, the milk has disappeared.

COMMENT

Support for the Revolution is neither uniform nor unanimous. It is in some cases greeted with 'stupidity' and 'apathy' (p. 10). Some animals still feel loyal to Jones. Mollie in particular seems keen to retain her privileges. Moses represents the role of the Church and organised religion. He is seen as a 'clever talker' (p. 10). He is another character whose command of language is seen as a dangerous skill. Jones's character is developed further as idle and self-indulgent.

What does Orwell's use of the word 'reveal' suggest about the pigs' learning?

The description of the farm after the revolution is poetic and contains an evocative physical description of the animals' activities. Why do the animals want to preserve the house as a museum? Their reluctance to enter it and their reaction to it emphasises the terror of Jones's reign.

MANOR FARM – A DREAM OF THE FUTURE

However, the animals do not all react to the house in the same way – Mollie admires herself in the mirror when she picks up Mrs Jones's blue ribbon. Her self-interest prevents her from understanding what the farm house symbolises to the other animals.

GLOSSARY   **linseed cake** a form of animal feed
Windsor Chair a wooden high-backed chair
castrate to remove the genitals
gambolled ran playfully
spinney small group of trees and bushes
looking-glasses mirrors

A Identify the speaker.

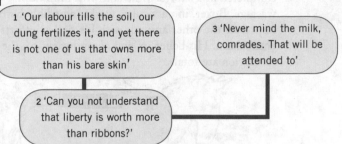

1 'Our labour tills the soil, our dung fertilizes it, and yet there is not one of us that owns more than his bare skin'

3 'Never mind the milk, comrades. That will be attended to'

2 'Can you not understand that liberty is worth more than ribbons?'

Identify the character 'to whom' this comment refers.

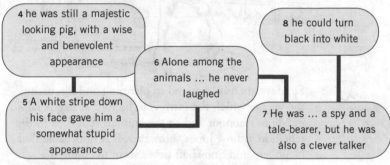

4 he was still a majestic looking pig, with a wise and benevolent appearance

8 he could turn black into white

6 Alone among the animals ... he never laughed

5 A white stripe down his face gave him a somewhat stupid appearance

7 He was ... a spy and a tale-bearer, but he was also a clever talker

Check your answers on page 88.

B Consider these issues.

a The picture that Major paints about the conditions of the animals' lives on the farm.

b How far the animals are prepared to sacrifice their privileges for the Rebellion.

c In what ways the author hints that some animals are already guilty of self-interest.

d How far Orwell determines the reader's approval of certain characters.

e What risks are involved in being 'a clever talker'.

AFTER THE REVOLUTION – THE FARM UNDER ATTACK

CHAPTER 3 The animals' harvest breaks all previous records – it is completed in a shorter time and with minimum wastage. Boxer, in particular, works incredibly hard and impresses the other animals with his tireless efforts and enthusiasm. His belief in, and commitment to, the revolution are total.

Sundays are now devoted to planning and discussing the way in which the farm is to be run. A flag is raised in Major's honour and to the animals that died in the rebellion against Jones. However, it is noticeable that Napoleon and Snowball never seem to come to a consensus at meetings and are engaged in separate tasks. Snowball runs his committees, whilst Napoleon educates the young puppies he is keeping separate from the other animals. It becomes apparent that the pigs have taken the milk and apples for themselves. Squealer justifies this act to the others convincing them that it is being done for the benefit of the animals.

COMMENT

Is 'brainwork' equal to physical labour? What do you think Orwell is suggesting here?

The equality that Major stressed as being so important in his meeting is jeopardised straight away. The pigs are seen as more intelligent than other animals and are quick to take on board Major's teachings, 'with their superior knowledge it was natural that they should assume the leadership' (p. 16). By becoming the farm's administrators, the pigs avoid physical work.

The idealism of Major's speech is continued in Orwell's description of the harvest. He paints a picture of a community in which each individual works his hardest to achieve the best results for the group – 'Not an animal on the farm had stolen so much as a mouthful' (p. 17). Their behaviour is unselfish and as a result they achieve greater success than they did before their cooperation. Much of the success of the harvest depends on Boxer's strength and total commitment, 'There were days when the entire work of the farm seemed to rest on his mighty shoulders' (p. 17). He is determined to work for the farm in contrast to Mollie and the cat who can best be described as parasites. They contribute little to life on the farm and appear to be only interested in what they can use for their own advantage.

Look at Orwell's use of the word 'duty' to suggest the pigs' motives.

Although the reader for much of this chapter sees events from the animals' point of view this is used for an ironic (see Literary Terms) purpose. The reader is aware of what is really taking place. The pigs' cleverness becomes a double-edged sword as it enables them to exploit the other animals. Boxer's physical strength and gentle nature mean that he is easy to manipulate.

List the advantages and disadvantages of debate.

The conflict between Snowball and Napoleon comes from their opposing views. Rather than negotiate or come to a consensus, decisions are increasingly imposed on the animals. The harmony and equality of farm life is being disrupted. Napoleon dismisses Snowball's work and concentrates instead on building up his own power. The reader is given some hints as to how this is done but its full extent is delayed until later in the novel.

Snowball's character appears to be that of an innovator. He organises various committees in an effort to help the animals, although we wonder how far this is meant

AFTER THE REVOLUTION – THE FARM UNDER ATTACK

Consider what Orwell's description of the animals' reading ability tells you about them.

to make them self-sufficient. The list of the committees he establishes becomes comical, suggesting that many of these are of little practical use to the animals. The most important aim is to promote literacy amongst the animals. Snowball is also seen in a less appealing light in this chapter. Look at his reaction when the windfall apples are taken and the fact that he agrees with the pigs' use of the milk. The animals 'assumed as a matter of course' (p. 21) that the windfalls would be shared out. How dangerous is it to make these assumptions?

Look at the use of the word 'order' on page 21.

One of the most significant characters is Squealer. We see here just how adept he is at persuading the animals. He defends the pigs' actions in a brilliant piece of rhetoric (see Literary Terms) which is underlined by the basic threat of Jones's return. Throughout the novel he systematically distorts Major's original commandments, reflecting the gradual erosion of the animals' high revolutionary ideals. The animals are given little option but to agree to the pigs' actions. Squealer becomes Napoleon's propagandist (see Political Terms).

GLOSSARY   **literate** able to read and write
                  windfalls apples that have fallen to the ground

CHAPTER 4   Mr Frederick and Mr Pilkington whose farms border Animal Farm are introduced. They become increasingly concerned about events at Animal Farm and worry in particular that their animals might revolt against them in a similar fashion. Rebellion is seen as spreading to other farms, where it is violently suppressed.

Jones makes a reappearance. He has become no more likable in his absence and is presented as a weak and ineffectual character. Jones's drunkenness is again referred to. He now spends most of his time in the pub.

Frederick and Pilkington invade Animal Farm hoping

Look at the roles each of the animals take in the battle.

to quell the animals there but are beaten by the farm animals who are brilliantly led by Snowball. The 'Battle of the Cowshed', as it becomes known, is to become a national holiday to commemorate the saving of the farm.

One of the main events in the novel is the 'Battle of the Cowshed'; it is Snowball's finest hour. His brilliant command of the animals, his careful planning and tactics and above all his own bravery in battle are crucial to the animals' success. He is the undisputed hero of the event.

COMMENT

The humans in the book are depicted as unpleasant. The farmers try to take advantage of Jones's situation. Man's brutality (as referred to by Major in his speech) is again reinforced with the cruel suppression of any signs of revolt on neighbouring farms. Pilkington and Frederick dislike each other and their self-interest prevents them from uniting successfully against Animal Farm. Their hypocrisy is later apparent when they trade with and are entertained by Napoleon. Indeed, the pigs are admired by them as they have surpassed their own unpleasantness and standards of exploitation.

How far does Snowball's reading of books contradict Major's commandments?

Snowball is a brilliant strategist. He anticipates the humans' attack and devises a carefully planned campaign in which the invaders are ambushed. His bravery in battle is also significant in terms of the way in which Napoleon will later twist the day's events. Boxer's humanity (in the best sense of the word) is emphasised when he is upset at knocking the stable-lad unconscious during the battle. In contrast to Snowball's ruthless dismissal of human suffering, 'The only good human is a dead human' (p. 27), Boxer is horrified that he might have hurt someone. He will work hard to achieve his goal but is not prepared for others to suffer. This again makes the reader warm to his character. His compassion and grief at his own actions contrast strongly with that of the pigs, as does his willingness to accept the blame for the injury when placed against the pigs' later willingness to excuse their every action. This further emphasises Boxer's heroic nature.

GLOSSARY
'had their females in common' shared their females. Originally the Communists opposed marriage
contemptible seen as worthless and despicable
smithies blacksmith's workplaces, where horseshoes are made
Julius Caesar a Roman emperor, renowned for his battle-plans

A *Identify the speaker.*

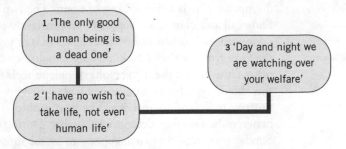

1 'The only good human being is a dead one'

2 'I have no wish to take life, not even human life'

3 'Day and night we are watching over your welfare'

Identify the character 'to whom' this comment refers.

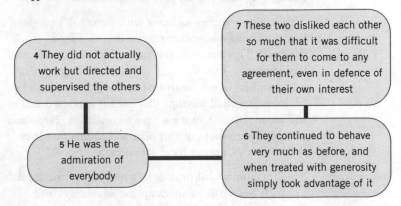

4 They did not actually work but directed and supervised the others

5 He was the admiration of everybody

6 They continued to behave very much as before, and when treated with generosity simply took advantage of it

7 These two disliked each other so much that it was difficult for them to come to any agreement, even in defence of their own interest

Check your answers on page 88.

B *Consider these issues.*

a How important physical strength is in itself.

b Whether Major's ideals are possible to achieve.

c How Squealer manages to convince the animals of the truth of his arguments and the techniques he uses.

THE STRUGGLE FOR POWER

CHAPTER 5

*Look at how
Mollie has
betrayed the
revolution.*

Mollie who has never really taken to the revolution or to the changed way of life under the animals, disappears. She is never spoken of again. The two pigs, Snowball and Napoleon, appear to be constantly at odds with each other: Snowball believes that to prevent the farm from further attack, pigeons should be sent to other farms to get them to revolt. Napoleon feels that this should only happen once they have sufficient firearms to defend themselves. The relationship between the two pigs deteriorates rapidly. During the Sunday meetings, Snowball appears to be the most popular as a result of his eloquent speeches. Napoleon is building up his own support at other times.

This conflict reaches a climax with Snowball's proposal that the animals now concentrate on building a windmill. This becomes central to the issue of who will lead the farm. The windmill holds out the promise of a future similar in nature to that given to the animals by Major – Snowball predicts that once it is operational it will mean that the animals have to work less. Napoleon strongly disapproves of this plan and claims that they should firstly improve food production.

*How useful are
these speeches if
the animals don't
understand them?*

This antagonism culminates in a meeting of the animals in which Snowball balances up the advantages and disadvantages of his plans for the windmill and tries to convince the animals through rational argument. Whilst the animals are convinced by his speech, it seems that they barely grasp its meaning.

Napoleon after an especially short and brutal speech utters a terrifying sound, 'like a war cry', summoning his dogs to chase Snowball from the farm. The attack is clearly preplanned. The farm animals are terrified by the arrival of the dogs and after the attack they are cowed and frightened. Napoleon takes this opportunity to announce that all future Sunday meetings will be

Orwell's detached tone when describing this event emphasises the extraordinary nature of this event.

abolished. The animals' loss of control over the way in which they are governed becomes apparent. The animals are told by Squealer that Snowball is a traitor and has been working against them.

At a later meeting, Napoleon states that the plans for the windmill will go ahead after all, surprising the animals with his change of decision. They do not notice Napoleon's introduction of a further reduction in rationing.

Squealer again explains Napoleon's actions. This time, however, he is accompanied by three dogs who intimidate the animals into agreement.

COMMENT   Even before Snowball's expulsion and Napoleon's cancellation of the debates, it is clear that the pigs now control what happens on the farm; they now decide 'all questions of farm policy' (p. 29). At first they claim that this still has to be agreed by a vote and passed by the majority but eventually all decisions are taken by the pigs. This demonstrates the slow erosion of the farm animals' grip upon their lives.

The differences between the two pigs are clear. Snowball has many schemes – which in theory would improve the life of the animals but would take some effort to put into practice, such as his plan for the windmill. His schemes seem to be for the farm's benefit rather than for his own. Napoleon is seen to have little time for such plans – nor indeed respect for those who make them. This is most apparent in his urinating on Snowball's plans which emphasises again his brutal and uncivilised character. Animals urinate on objects to mark their territory. This is symbolic as Napoleon later takes the idea for the windmill as his own. On the allegorical level (see Literary Terms) the differing views of socialism held by Trotsky and Stalin are apparent (see Themes). In contrast with Snowball's speeches,

THE STRUGGLE FOR POWER

Napoleon merely makes the minimum response and when he does speak it is usually to criticise Snowball. It is clear that Napoleon's campaign against him is carefully planned. Speech becomes less and less important to Napoleon. The sheep with their mindless bleating effectively silence opposing opinions as no-one else can be heard.

Note the occasions *when the sheep* *start bleating.*

Plans are simplified into slogans rather than discussed in reasoned speeches. It is clear such speeches are beyond the intelligence of most of the animals. The way in which the rest of the farm animals come to change their mind according to whoever is speaking emphasises the fickle nature of the crowd and their lack of intelligence which again leaves them open to exploitation. For all his intelligence, Snowball is unaware of the manner in which Napoleon is building up power against him. Whilst he advocates the use of the pigeons' propaganda (see Political Terms) abroad (and clearly benefits from Squealer's propaganda regarding the apples and milk) he becomes the victim of propaganda himself as Napoleon seeks to consolidate his position.

The way in which the animals have deviated from Major's ideals is apparent in the gradual way in which the figure of Napoleon himself becomes more and more important. He takes over Major's status by standing on the platform where Major gave his speech.

With the cancellation of the debates, any pretence of consensus is gone. The Sunday meetings instead of being a time when the animals agree their workload becomes the assembly at which their orders are given. Their freedom to act and live as they wish is gone. They are under the pigs' control. None of the animals challenge the decisions that are made. They passively accept them. The four porkers who try to protest are easily gagged. In this way, the animals are part of the system that silences them, making them even easier for the pigs to manipulate. They collaborate unknowingly in their downfall.

Snowball's exile and Napoleon's use of terror effectively remove all opposition to the latter's plans. The unquestioning obedience of the dogs emphasises the way in which the pigs come increasingly to resemble man in his worst aspects. The use of violence and intimidation marks a watershed in the novel. The terror of the other animals and their lack of comprehension at what has happened emphasises the distance the animals have travelled since they first listened to Major's speech. Napoleon will resort to force and violence increasingly as he attempts to establish absolute power over the animals. After this, all hope of a more just and equitable society are made less likely as the regime on the farm becomes increasingly violent and thus more powerful. The farm is now on its way to becoming a totalitarian society (see Political Terms) which is governed by intimidation, terror and ignorance.

List the ways in which Squealer casts doubt on the animals' beliefs in these two chapters.

Squealer's propaganda is crucial to Napoleon. He depicts Napoleon in a heroic mould (Napoleon is said to have 'deep and heavy responsibilities' and to have made 'sacrifices' – p. 35) and emphasises the gulf between the animals and their leader. By his skilful use of omissions and half-truths – not to mention outright lies, Squealer succeeds in convincing the animals of Napoleon's fitness for power and the validity of his methods. The animals do not understand the meaning of the word 'tactics' but do not question it.

GLOSSARY   **ratified** formally agreed
                    procured obtained
                    sordid unpleasant
                    disinterred dug up

THE STRUGGLE FOR POWER

CHAPTER 6 Life under the pigs at Animal Farm is increasingly harsh. In an effort to build the windmill as quickly as possible the animals work harder than ever, even on Sundays (which had previously been a day of rest). The work is difficult and slow. Boxer works persistently to complete it and asks to be woken early.

The animals are shocked and surprised to learn that Napoleon has started to trade with other farms. The animals at first have doubts but are won over by Squealer who quickly persuades them that this is not against the principles of Animalism. Squealer uses the animals' lack of literacy against them when defending Napoleon. He asks whether their records are written down anywhere and plays on their faith in the pigs. He does this again when the pigs break the Fourth Commandment by moving into the farmhouse and sleeping on beds. He convinces the animals that their welfare is dependent on the pigs' well-being: otherwise Jones would return.

Napoleon begins to elevate himself above the other pigs by the use of the title 'Leader'. The pigs are clearly breaking the guidelines that Major gave them.

After all their work, the animals are appalled to find

Look back to Major's speech and consider what he would have said about a death sentence.

that the windmill has been destroyed in a gale. Napoleon tells the animals that this was not caused by the storm but was an act of sabotage by Snowball, who is apparently trying to destroy their work from Foxwood Farm. He shows the animals the evidence of Snowball's trot-prints and passes the death sentence on him.

COMMENT

Orwell's use of irony (see Literary Terms) directs the reader's attention as to what is really happening in the novel. The description of the animals as 'working like slaves' and their pride that their work is not for an 'idle pack of humans' (p. 37) is undercut by the reader's awareness that the animals are being exploited in exactly this way by the pigs.

The issue of how opposition is to be organised if one lacks the words to express it is a theme in Orwell's later novel 1984.

The pigs' use – or rather misuse – language to make the sufferings that they inflict upon the animals sound acceptable. The labour that the animals do is said to be voluntary but it is actually compulsory: if the animals don't work, they will not be fed. This distortion of language will become more obvious as the story proceeds. (See also the Theme on language.)

The animals are seen to suffer as a result of their labour. Boxer is losing his super-human strength. He refuses to reduce his pace however, despite Clover's warnings and continues to overwork. His belief in the revolution appears to be as strong as ever but the reader increasingly questions how wise he is to trust Napoleon, whom, it is clear, does not have the farm's best interests at heart. It is clear by now that such faith is misplaced and dangerous. Animals like Boxer increasingly resort to slogans and mottoes (see Literary Terms) – 'I will work harder' and 'Napoleon is always right' (p. 35). This has the effect of limiting the animals' thoughts. Their unquestioning obedience makes them easy prey for Squealer.

THE STRUGGLE FOR POWER

The animals feel 'a vague uneasiness' when this is announced (p. 39). Napoleon's announcement about the trading with other farms is a mere formality – the plans have already been made. Napoleon justifies his actions less and less. Having used terror to subdue the animals and now governing a docile and frightened farm, he can afford to be more open about his flouting of the rules of Animalism. By engaging in trade, Napoleon himself becomes a capitalist (see Political Terms).

Look at the use of the word 'evidence' as used by Squealer. Snowball's exile provides Napoleon with a scapegoat. If any of his plans fail, Snowball can be blamed. There is also less chance of any opposition: all the animals are united against a common enemy.

GLOSSARY   **traitor** someone who betrays their friends, country or beliefs

TEST YOURSELF (Chapters 5–6)

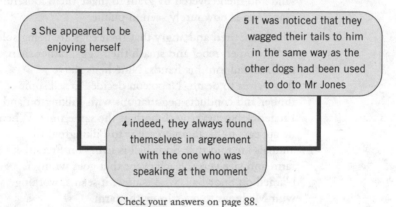

A ... *Identify the speaker.*

1 'He would be only too happy to let you make your decisions for yourselves'

2 'Do you know the enemy who has come in the night and overthrown our windmill?'

Identify the character 'to whom' this comment refers.

3 She appeared to be enjoying herself

5 It was noticed that they wagged their tails to him in the same way as the other dogs had been used to do to Mr Jones

4 indeed, they always found themselves in argreement with the one who was speaking at the moment

Check your answers on page 88.

B ... *Consider these issues.*

a Whether you agree with the statement 'Bravery is not enough. Loyalty and obedience are more important'.

b What methods Napoleon uses to remove opposition to him.

c How the animals' inability to think for themselves contributes to their own oppression.

d What hints there are in Chapters 5

and 6 that Napoleon has carefully planned the way he gains power.

e What Orwell's use of the phrase 'was sent' suggests and how his use of language shapes the reader's response to events in the novel.

f How the animals' opinion of Snowball has changed by the end of Chapter 6.

NAPOLEON AND THE REIGN OF TERROR

CHAPTER 7

The animals suffer a period of severe hardship as winter approaches. In contrast to their earlier dreams of plenty and abundance, the animals now face starvation. The windmill is rebuilt (this time with thicker walls) but work is slow.

Rumours of starvation on Animal Farm begin to spread to the other farms. Napoleon takes Mr Whymper, the farm agent, around the farm to show him that the rumours are untrue but the food bins are filled with sand and then covered by grain to make them look full. Napoleon is now rarely seen in public.

The hens, tired and angry that their eggs are being sold to Whymper, rebel and smash their eggs, rather than let them fall into his hands. Nine hens starve themselves to death. Napoleon decides to sell some timber and conducts negotiations with Pilkington and Frederick but never with both at the same time. When he appears to be about to sell it to Pilkington, the animals are told that Snowball is living on Frederick's farm and vice versa. Each event that goes wrong is blamed on Snowball, who is now, it seems, working with Mr Jones to overthrow the farm.

A new phase is reached when the four pigs, who protested about the cancellation of the Sunday meeting, and the three hens who led the rebellion over the eggs are executed in front of the other (now extremely frightened) animals. The farm animals are terrified by the massacre and gather, huddling together, on the Knoll. They are then told that the singing of 'Beasts of England' is banned. Life on the farm is becoming increasingly oppressive.

Note the use of the word 'Comrade'. Look at the use of the word by Major at the start of the novel.

An official poet, Minimus, composes an alternative anthem and in Chapter 8 a poem of praise to Comrade Napoleon. It is a worthless piece of work but because its message is one that Napoleon agrees with, it is accepted and promoted by the pigs.

COMMENT — Napoleon tricks the other farmers into believing that the animals live in a happy and contented state and that food is plentiful. The animals never reflect on the way in which they have been tricked into accepting rationing by the pigs. The possibility of a rebellion against Napoleon becomes apparent when the hens refuse to hand over their eggs for sale, something Major had spoken against (see p. 4) and which the hens see as murder. Napoleon's ruthlessness is apparent in the way in which he starves and suppresses them.

The collapse of the windmill is blamed on Snowball. Having taken the credit for the plans and design of the structure Napoleon cannot be seen to fail. Throughout this chapter, Snowball is used as a shadowy figure intent on ruining the farm. An atmosphere of hysteria is created whereby the animals will confess to having committed the most ridiculous crimes, providing Napoleon with a ready-made excuse to hunt down any opposition to him. Napoleon creates a 'cult' around him. He is rarely seen and is now referred to as 'Our Leader, Comrade Napoleon' (p. 51). Instead of the 'real' Napoleon, Squealer gives the animals an image of a heroic leader whose wisdom can never be questioned. Napoleon is said to be a brave and successful fighter. He awards himself medals and his appearances become mainly ceremonial. Squealer becomes more and more important as the only means of communication between Napoleon and the other animals. Even the most stupid of the animals question the executions but Squealer is again able to answer them. The animals' trust in him is another reason for his success. He becomes a sinister figure in this chapter, giving Boxer 'a very ugly look' (p. 51) when the horse questions his criticism of Snowball. Boxer is later attacked by the dogs, suggesting that Squealer has identified him as a possible threat and marked him down for elimination.

Look at Napoleon's actions at the 'Battle of the Cowshed'. Does he deserve his medals?

Look at Squealer's account of the 'Battle of the Cowshed' and that given in the book on page 50.

Even Napoleon's most loyal supporter, Boxer, is not free from attack. Incredibly, having defended himself from attack by the dogs, he looks to Napoleon to tell him what to do. His unquestioning obedience suggests one reason why the revolution has failed. It never occurs to Boxer that Napoleon's attack on him has been deliberate and premeditated.

Compare how the different animals react to the executions.

The executions that Napoleon organises parallel Stalin's bloody suppression of any opposition to him during the 1920s and 1930s (see Theme on the Russian Revolution). Napoleon's elimination of his opponents becomes a massacre. We see Napoleon as a dictator and a tyrant. The hens' rebellion is quickly quashed and he eliminates anyone who does not support him. His rule becomes more absolute and contradicts Major's instruction that all animals are equal. The executions end any hope that the revolution might succeed or that there is any chance for equality and freedom under Napoleon. The bloodbath is seen as worse than any under Jones (see p. 53). Nevertheless, the animals appear to believe that those executed were traitors. The animals appear to be numbed by the executions. They return to the Knoll, perhaps looking for the security that remembering the revolution would give them. Clover, who we have seen at the start as a maternal figure, is herself a source of comfort for the other animals. However she too is unable to think or voice her objections to what has just happened.

The chapter finishes with Orwell shifting from his use of the third person narrative (see Literary Terms) to that of one of the characters. We are given Clover's unconscious thoughts and feelings after a poetic description of the farm. She is numb and unable to express these thoughts but they demonstrate just how far the animals have been betrayed. We see that she is unable to protest through her fear and confusion.

Surprisingly, she still trusts the pigs and is loyal to
them.

Why do the
animals, even
though they doubt
the pigs, fail to
protest?

The detailed description of the farm and the emphasis
on its beauty is used by Orwell to create an image of
what the farm could be. He juxtaposes two different
visions, the ideal of the possible freedom and peace that
the animals could have achieved, against the terrifying
reality of their lives. In this way the reader is in no
doubt about the way in which the pigs have perverted
Major's ideas. The animals lose not only the ability to
voice their own thoughts, they are also deprived of their
song. As they 'lacked the words' (p. 54) to express their
real feelings, the animals start to sing 'Beasts of
England'. The song becomes a substitute for language
as the animals cannot form an articulate protest.
Squealer announces that it is banned; with its references
to a better world, it could be seen as subversive (see
Political Terms).

GLOSSARY

chaff thin straw or hay

pretext excuse

capitulated surrendered

collaborated worked with someone else as a traitor

secreted hidden

CHAPTER 8 The animals check the wall to remind themselves of the
Sixth Commandment and are surprised to find that it
now reads: 'No animal shall kill any other animal
without cause' (p. 56).

Squealer counters the animals' growing mistrust of
Napoleon by telling them that despite evidence to the
contrary, food production is increasing. The windmill is
at last completed and the animals celebrate their
expectation that now – at last – their life on the farm
will cease to be one of drudgery and labour.
After justifying his proposed selling of timber to

Pilkington by spreading rumours of Frederick's brutal treatment of the animals, Napoleon finally sells the timber to Frederick and the pigs congratulate themselves on their newly found business acumen. They then realise that they have been paid in forged notes. Frederick attacks the farm and blows up the windmill.

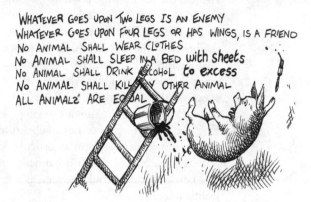

WHATEVER GOES UPON TWO LEGS IS AN ENEMY
WHATEVER GOES UPON FOUR LEGS OR HAS WINGS, IS A FRIEND
NO ANIMAL SHALL WEAR CLOTHES
NO ANIMAL SHALL SLEEP IN A BED *with sheets*
NO ANIMAL SHALL DRINK ALCOHOL *to excess*
NO ANIMAL SHALL KILL ANY OTHER ANIMAL
ALL ANIMALS ARE EQUAL

The animals are stunned by the loss of all that they have worked for and it is again Boxer who sets the example by immediately insisting that he will work harder than ever to rebuild it. This is an even greater effort for him, as he is not as strong as he once was. The pigs discover a crate of whisky and celebrate the selling of the timber to Frederick by getting drunk (it is encouraging to notice their hangovers the next morning!). Squealer is discovered after he collapses by the barn wall. The animals later notice that the Fifth Commandment now states that: 'No animal shall drink alcohol *to excess*' (p. 68).

COMMENT   Orwell begins several chapters with the extent of the animals' suffering on the farm. It is clear here that the animals' situation is unchanged. They 'fed no better than they had done in Jones's day' (p. 56). However, Napoleon is now living in considerable luxury. His lifestyle clearly contradicts Major's assertion that 'all the

habits of Man are evil' (p. 6). His status is further
enhanced by the titles that are now invented for him.
His vanity is obvious when he names the mill after
himself. The poem 'Comrade Napoleon' is bitterly
ironic (see Literary Terms) in view of the farm animals'
hunger and exhaustion.

Compare the two
extracts (pp. 25–7
and pp. 62–6).
See if you can
detect shift in
Orwell's mood,
particularly at the
end of the battles.

Napoleon's use of rumour when selling the timber
shows the way in which his regime is being held in
place by lies and half-truths. It also adds to the
sense of tension on the farm. Snowball is again
used as a scapegoat for any misfortune. The
gander's suicide marks yet another death on the
farm.

The 'Battle of the Windmill' is one of the few times we
now see the animals fighting for a common cause.
Their actions contrast sharply with those at the 'Battle
of the Cowshed'. Squealer's complete misrepresentation
of the 'Battle of the Windmill' shows that the pigs'
distortion of events is becoming complete. Now it is
not only events in the distant past which are altered but
recent history too. The celebrations following the Battle
are used to divert the animals' attention from the forged
banknotes.

Compare the
differences in
leadership between
Napoleon and
Snowball in the
two battles.

At the start of the novel we have seen that Jones is
incapable of running the farm as he is drunk and this is
later referred to as a reason why he is unfit to win back
the farm. The pigs imitate man by drinking alcohol and
suffer as a result. The fact that the hangover is blamed
on Snowball and that Napoleon feels himself to be
close to death, are seen by the reader as ridiculous
moments which although comic, suggest the pigs' lack
of accountability and eagerness to shift the blame for
any action onto others' heads. The pigs' later decision
to use the land set aside for retirement to grow grain
that they can distil for alcohol shows the extent of their

selfishness and their disregard for the happiness of the other animals on the farm.

Orwell makes an obvious use of irony (see Literary Terms) in the last paragraph of the chapter. To the animals the discovery of Squealer, collapsed with a pot of paint and a brush at the foot of the wall is a 'strange incident which hardly anyone was able to understand' (p. 67). To the reader it is clear that Squealer has been altering the Commandments as the pigs have broken them. It is through the use of the third person narrative (see Literary Terms) that Orwell is able gradually to reveal the animals' ignorance of their situation. That the animals find the discovery of Squealer unremarkable shows the reader just how unwilling the animals are to trust the evidence of their own eyes. They are now so used to having others think for them that they are unable to do this for themselves.

CHAPTER 9   Boxer's hoof which was injured in the 'Battle of the Windmill' is taking a long time to heal and causes him great pain.

The impending winter results in increased food shortages and hardship for the animals. Squealer continues to produce lists of statistics which claim that life on the farm has improved dramatically since Jones left.

Napoleon's four sows produce thirty-one piglets and it is decided that they will be educated in their own school-room.

What is a republic? Would you describe Animal Farm as one?

Napoleon orders Spontaneous Demonstrations to show support and declares the farm to be a Republic, with himself, of course, as President (see Political Terms).

Boxer collapses, unable to continue his work and the pigs claim that they have sent him to a hospital to recover. As the van pulls out of the farm, Benjamin realises that Boxer is in fact being sold to the knacker's yard and the animals try to get Boxer to kick himself free. He is so weak he is unable to do so and is driven off to his death. Squealer denies this and tells the animals that Boxer died painlessly and in comfort.

The pigs spend the money they earn on his corpse by buying another crate of whisky and hold a memorial banquet in his honour.

COMMENT

Look at the reference to the pigs' tails on page 70. Compare this with what Snowball told Mollie about ribbons in Chapter 2.

The rumours about the use of an area of pasture for retired animals shows how much the animals rely on rumour rather than fact for information about their lives. Squealer's distortion of the truth and language becomes almost farcical when he claims that 'A too rigid equality in rations ... would have been contrary to the principles of Animalism' (p. 69). This completely distorts the meaning of the word 'equality', reducing language to nonsense. His statistics also completely misrepresent the reality of life on the farm. The farm's inequality is clear in the comparison between the hungry and cold animals, whose lives are 'harsh and bare' (p. 69) and the pigs, who 'were putting on weight if anything' (p. 70).

The pigs divert attention from the animals' increasing hardship through the use of parades, songs and propaganda (see Political Terms). Moses returns to the farm with tales of Sugar Candy Mountain. The pigs' reaction to this is very different from earlier in the novel. He is fed by the pigs in exactly the same way that Jones fed them.

Boxer's hoof provides another significant moment in the novel. It is one of the first times we see Benjamin's devotion to his friend but we also realise how much Boxer has sacrificed to bring about Major's vision. Boxer's eventual departure in the van is a horrifying moment as the reader is aware of the pigs' total

NAPOLEON AND THE REIGN OF TERROR

indifference to the suffering of those who have helped them gain power. The fact that the most loyal and kind animal on the farm is sent by them to his death emphasises again the ruthless nature of the pigs' regime. The animals' inability to help until it is too late suggests that events would never had taken this turn had they been more involved at the start of the revolution instead of allowing the pigs to take control. The fact that the pigs use the money they have gained as the result of Boxer's death on alcohol is obscene and demonstrates their unfitness to govern. Major's prophecy has been fulfilled and it is perhaps the strongest indictment of the pigs' rule that they murder their most loyal follower.

The penultimate chapter demonstrates the range of privileges the pigs have now acquired. The increased elitism of the farm is marked by the fact that the young pigs are kept apart from the other animals. Both the pigs and dogs have better rations than the other animals and will be taught in the new school-house that is being built for them by the other animals. They are being trained to be leaders and to continue the dominance of the pigs over the other animals. The prospects for the future look bleak as even if Napoleon died, other pigs are ready to assume the leadership.

A *Identify the speaker.*

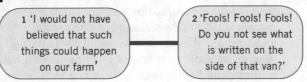

1 'I would not have believed that such things could happen on our farm'

2 'Fools! Fools! Fools! Do you not see what is written on the side of that van?'

Identify the character 'to whom' this comment refers.

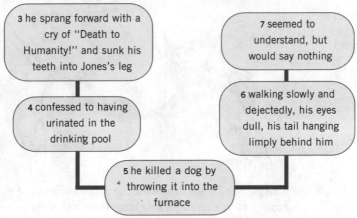

3 he sprang forward with a cry of "Death to Humanity!" and sunk his teeth into Jones's leg

7 seemed to understand, but would say nothing

4 confessed to having urinated in the drinking pool

6 walking slowly and dejectedly, his eyes dull, his tail hanging limply behind him

5 he killed a dog by throwing it into the furnace

Check your answers on page 88.

B *Consider these issues.*

a In what ways life on the farm has altered since Chapter 3.

b Why the animals accept Squealer's version of the 'Battle of the Cowshed'.

c How Orwell builds up the atmosphere of hysteria and terror in these three chapters.

d Whether you agree with Benjamin's behaviour in refusing to get involved in the events around him, although he clearly understands the true nature of Napoleon's rule.

THE DREAM BETRAYED

Who benefits from the farm's increased prosperity?

The final chapter of the book looks at the farm many years later. Few of the old animals still survive and the farm is mainly occupied by younger animals who vaguely believe in Animalism but don't really understand it. The second windmill has been built and in some ways the farm is now more prosperous but the animals work harder than ever (all talk of retirement has long since vanished and no animal has retired).

The pigs and dogs deal with the administration of the farm. Clover's terrified neighing alerts the older animals. They are horrified to see Squealer walking on two legs. He is followed by a long line of pigs, all doing the same thing. Napoleon then leaves the farmhouse, again, walking on two legs, carrying a whip in his trotter. This is in complete defiance of Major's teachings. The animals' world has been turned 'upside-down' (p. 83).

The description of the pigs leaving the farmhouse is sinister enough in itself. They take part in an unnatural action, one which flatly contradicts the First Commandment.

In addition, all the Commandments have been erased. In their place is a single slogan:

ALL ANIMALS ARE EQUAL

BUT SOME ANIMALS ARE MORE

EQUAL THAN OTHERS

The next day all the pigs who supervise the animals at work carry whips.

The pigs behave more and more like humans: buying newspapers, smoking and wearing clothes. They even invite their human neighbours to dinner. The other farmers congratulate the pigs on the way they have managed to make more money out of the farm than Jones ever did while, at the same time, giving the animals even less food and comfort. The older animals look through the window, as the quarrel between Napoleon and Mr Pilkington erupts (both have cheated at cards). The animals are appalled to see that they can no longer distinguish between the faces of the humans and the animals. The transformation is complete.

COMMENT

Napoleon states that 'The truest happiness … lay in working hard and living frugally' (p. 80). Is this true of the pigs?

Many of the original animals have now died. The newer members of the farm have little understanding of the revolution or of its aims. Opposition to the pigs is weakened even further as fewer animals remember the revolution's original aims. The outlook for the future looks hopeless at the end of this chapter. The windmill is complete but the life of the animals is no easier than before. Again, the only animals who seem to benefit from it are the pigs. Despite the fact that none of their hoped-for benefits have arrived, the animals still hope that some day they will be free and described as patriotic. The animals still believe that they are privileged and equal. In this way Orwell shows the way in which they have deluded themselves and thus helped others to control them.

THE DREAM BETRAYED

The removal of the Seven Commandments and the imposition of the nonsensical slogan 'All Animals Are Equal But Some Are More Equal Than Others' shows how thoroughly the revolution has been perverted. After this, the pigs' descent into human behaviour and actions is rapid. The horrified neighing of Clover alerts the reader to the total corruption of Major's ideas by the pigs. The fact that Napoleon carries a whip in his 'hand' – seen at the opening of the novel as a symbol of man's vicious oppression of the animals – suggests the form that the animals' future will take. The sheep now bleat 'Four legs good. Two legs *better*' showing how unthinking support can silence opposition but also how easy it is for the pigs to manipulate the other animals.

List the methods used by Orwell to arouse the reader's indignation and horror in this chapter.

The transformation of Napoleon in this novel into a man becomes complete. He is seen wearing Jones's clothes, his favourite sow one of Mrs Jones's dresses. It is clear that in comparison to the suffering of the other animals, the pigs are living in comparative luxury. The arrival of humans on the farm emphasises again the complete reversal of every one of Major's instructions. Far from having nothing to do with man, the pigs are now entertaining him. In fact, they have surpassed him, as is clear when the farmers congratulate Napoleon on managing to run a farm in a crueller way than even they do. The pigs have thus become even more evil than man.

We see the final scene in the book through Clover's eyes. This is the second time she has been used to give the reader an insight into events in the novel. That the pigs are worse than the system that they have replaced is due to the way in which they have systematically broken the commandments and betrayed and abused the trust that the other animals had placed in them. Major's hopes of a free and equal society have been seen to be just as he described them – a dream.

A *Identify the speaker.*

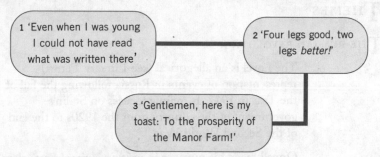

1 'Even when I was young I could not have read what was written there'

2 'Four legs good, two legs *better!*'

3 'Gentlemen, here is my toast: To the prosperity of the Manor Farm!'

Identify the character 'to whom' this comment refers.

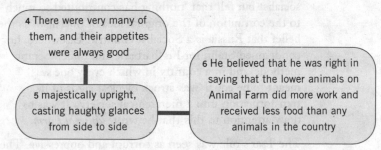

4 There were very many of them, and their appetites were always good

5 majestically upright, casting haughty glances from side to side

6 He believed that he was right in saying that the lower animals on Animal Farm did more work and received less food than any animals in the country

Check your answers on page 88.

B *Consider these issues.*

a Whether you agree with Benjamin that 'hunger, hardship, and disappointment' are part of the 'unalterable law of life' (p. 81). If this is so, what hope might there be for change.

b To what extent is criticism vital to society.

c How important education is in *Animal Farm*.

d In what ways (by the end of Chapter 10) the farm is similar to the description of the farm under Mr Jones.

PART THREE

COMMENTARY

THEMES

THE RUSSIAN REVOLUTION

The novel is an allegorical (see Literary Terms) representation of events in Russia following the fall of the Tsar in 1917. It mainly focuses on Stalin's government of the country from the 1920s to the end of the Second World War.

Orwell made his purpose in writing *Animal Farm* clear in his Preface to the Ukrainian edition. He was a socialist but felt that 'nothing has contributed so much to the corruption of the original idea of Socialism as the belief that Russia is a Socialist country'. Elsewhere, he condemned Stalin for his 'barbaric and undemocratic methods' and in a country in which every one was meant to be equal 'was struck by clear signs of its transformation into a hierarchical society'. It was to draw attention to this that he wrote *Animal Farm*.

The Tsar's rule was seen as corrupt and oppressive. The revolution of 1917 brought the Communists, under Lenin to power. Russia was now known as the USSR (Union of Soviet Socialist Republics) or the Soviet Union.

By comparing Marx's ideas to Major's speech, Orwell demonstrates how Stalin corrupted Marx and Lenin's socialist ideas.

Communism (which appears in the novel as 'Animalism') was based on the teachings of Karl Marx, a German philosopher. He believed that the ordinary working population were exploited by a minority of wealthy people who owned the factories and farms on which the workers laboured. The workers themselves (or the proletariat as Marx called them – see Political Terms) did not enjoy the rewards of their labour. In fact they were often treated harshly and earned low

wages so that the capitalists made a greater profit. Marx
believed that this was unfair and predicted that workers
would one day turn against their employers and create a
world in which all people were equal.

These ideas became part of the *Communist Manifesto*
and they provide the basis for Major's speech in
Chapter 1. The need for freedom, justice and equality is
stressed throughout the passage, as is the need for
revolution.

*Look at the ways
in which these
European
countries are
presented in the
novel.*

The Russian Revolution was greeted with alarm by
other countries in Europe. Their governments were very
worried at the possibility that communism would
spread and that they would face the same fate as the
Tsar. As a result, when supporters of the Tsar (known
as the Whites) mounted opposition to the
Communists, several countries sent forces into Russia
to destroy Lenin's government and help the Tsar regain
power. The Communists won the Civil War aided by
Trotsky's inspired leadership of the Red Army – a clear
parallel is made with Orwell's reference to Jones's
invasion and the 'Battle of the Cowshed'. The animals
win the battle as the result of Snowball's brilliant
planning.

After the Civil War, Lenin was determined to
modernise the Soviet Union. His death in 1924 resulted
in a struggle for power between Trotsky and Stalin,
reflected in the book in the disagreements between
Snowball and Napoleon. The two men disagreed on the
way in which the country should be modernised.
Trotsky thought that the development of industry was
most important whilst Stalin felt that they should
concentrate on agriculture.

Another issue was that of defence. Trotsky advocated
'Permanent Revolution', believing that the revolution
had to be spread to other countries so that the Soviet

Union was not isolated as the only communist country. Stalin opposed this policy and called for the Soviet Union to build up its defences first ('Socialism in one Country'), so that they would be prepared for any further foreign attacks. These debates mirror those in the novel over the issues of the windmill and the defence of the farm. Stalin eventually seized power and Trotsky was exiled in 1924. He was later murdered on Stalin's orders.

The suffering of the Soviet people throughout this period is reflected in the emphasis on hardwork and hard conditions that the animals experience in the novel.

Once in power, Stalin attempted to industrialise the Soviet Union through the introduction of 'Five Year Plans'. Unrealistically high production targets were set for workers – one miner, Alexander Stakhanov produced fourteen times his quota in one five hour shift. This was then set as the norm. Farms were to be collectivised (i.e. put under the control of the state) and although Stalin claimed that this was voluntary, it was forced upon the the Soviet people. Collectivisation was so unpopular that many farmers (like the hens who destroyed their eggs) killed their cattle and destroyed their farms rather than let them fall into government hands. This resulted in famines during the 1930s. It has been estimated by Western historians that between ten and fifteen million peasants died as a result of these famines.

Daily life in the Soviet Union for many was harsh but this deteriorated further when Stalin began to hunt down anyone who could possibly challenge his authority. Orwell's description of Napoleon's suppression of those who disagreed with him and the executions in Chapter 7 are clearly based on Stalin's 'purges'. No area of society was safe and anyone who was considered to be critical of Stalin in any way was either deported to forced labour camps in Siberia or executed. Of the 1,996 Communist Party delegates in 1934, 1,108 were executed in the following three years.

Half of the commissioned officer corps of the Russian army, which totalled around 35,000 men, were imprisoned or shot. Innocent people were accused of crimes and placed on 'trial'. These 'show trials' were given their name as the victims often confessed to their guilt as the result of brainwashing or of threats to their family. The results of many of the trials were a forgone conclusion anyway, as few escaped execution. A common allegation at these trials was that the accused had been working with Trotsky to overthrow the state.

The Soviet Union had always felt vulnerable to attack. In particular both Britain and Germany were seen as enemies. In 1939, as the Second World War began, Stalin signed a Non-aggression Pact with Hitler which he hoped would ensure that the country would not be attacked by Germany. This is symbolised in the novel as Napoleon's bargaining with Frederick and Pilkington over the timber. Despite this treaty, Hitler invaded in 1941 and got as far as Moscow before being defeated. Russian losses in this war were horrific. In 1943, the Soviet Union formed an alliance with Britain and the United States at the Tehran Conference. Orwell predicted that this friendship would not last and closed his novel with a scene based on the conference. His prediction proved accurate when the Cold War, a prolonged period of antagonism between the Soviet Union and the West, began in the late 1940s.

Napoleon is in some ways worse than Mr Jones as the pig has betrayed the animals' trust in him.

The Seven Commandments are gradually destroyed or corrupted as the novel proceeds. They represent for Orwell the gradual perversion of Marx's original socialist ideas by Stalin over his period in power. So total is this corruption, that, like the pigs and men, at the end of the novel, Stalin is indistinguishable from the corrupt order he overthrew.

POWER CORRUPTS

The novel can also be taken as a more general attack on and analysis of the search for power and the way in which corrupt figures can gain and manipulate power for their own purposes.

The opposite to a utopian society is a distopian one. Animal Farm is clearly the latter.

Animal Farm is a satire (see Literary Terms) on political power. Lord Acton observed that: 'power corrupts and absolute power corrupts absolutely'. As the pigs gain power, it accordingly becomes harder and harder for them to resist the temptations of enjoying an easier life for themselves – especially as the other animals are too gullible to prevent themselves being manipulated. Orwell ridicules the pretence of such a society that it is in any way fair or equal.

In *Animal Farm*, Major's speech presents us with a utopia, a perfect society, but we see that putting such a society into practice is harder. The dependence of the revolution on individuals proves to be a fundamental stumbling-block. However, leaders are needed if a revolution is to succeed.

Orwell encourages the reader to consider whether we should always trust our political leaders.

The idea of equality is in itself difficult. During Major's speech the dogs have to be prevented from attacking the rats and the pigs assume their normal position at the front of the barn. From the start of the novel, the revolution is led by these animals. Orwell repeats the fact that they are the most intelligent animals on the farm several times throughout the book. The pigs are the only animals who can read or write fluently and once they have gained power, the temptations to exploit the less intelligent animals are obvious. Napoleon and the pigs take advantage of the faith and trust of the other animals. Animals like Boxer perform all the difficult and slow tasks whilst the pigs confine themselves to the far less demanding task of 'organising' or 'managing' the work.

The start of the novel presents the reader with a society in which equality would be difficult to achieve, but equality becomes much less likely once Napoleon seizes power.

Note the methods Orwell suggests are used by dictators to gain and maintain power.

That this is not a simple matter of self-indulgence becomes clear with the emergence of Napoleon as leader of the farm. His is a slow descent into tyranny. He is driven by power and throughout the novel is planning how to take it. We see this first when he takes control of the food in Chapter 2. His removal of the puppies to 'educate' them results in the creation of his own secret police. Napoleon uses the dogs to terrify the animals into obedience. Neither Squealer nor Napoleon is seen without their dogs, who growl menacingly whenever the animals ask difficult questions.

The abolition of debates and elections removes a valuable way of the animals expressing their opinions. Napoleon sees voting as irrelevant and it is easily suppressed by him. The bloodbath in the barn and the subsequent executions that follow, remind us of the most primitive and probably most effective way of maintaining power – terror. This use of murder and intimidation to keep control of absolute power goes completely against the ideas of the revolution.

One of the ways in which power is achieved and secured is by the careful management of all sources of information. The pigs make sound use of this throughout the novel and use it as a cloak to hide their acquisition of power and luxury. Napoleon makes use of Squealer's abilities to turn 'black into white' (p. 9) to brainwash the farm animals into accepting his decisions and actions. We see this when Squealer defends Napoleon's decision to build the windmill in Chapter 5 and the way in which he praises Napoleon's wisdom, kindness and judgement throughout the book.

Orwell suggests
that our own
memories are not
enough to protect
us against
sophisticated
propaganda. This
is also seen in his
later novel 1984.

In addition, history is rewritten to produce a more satisfactory account of the past for the dictator. In this way, Squealer completely misrepresents Snowball's actions during the 'Battle of the Cowshed' (p. 35) and glorifies Napoleon's supposed bravery when it was clear that he was a coward. The animals are therefore reliant upon their own memories which (as the results of Squealer's persuasion and partial truths) become less and less reliable. The lack of any other source of information means that they have no other way of checking the truth of Squealer's speeches. This false history becomes part of the present as any potential opponents are also accused of working with the traitor, Snowball, however unlikely this may appear.

Napoleon's farm by the end of the novel clearly resembles a totalitarian state. The animals have no control over any aspect of their lives and Napoleon's power over them is absolute. In this way, Orwell is not only identifying the way in which Stalin came to power in the Soviet Union but he is also giving a textbook account of how a dictator can grasp power.

Orwell seems to suggest that revolutions fail because their leaders, once in power, use power for their own ends. As they control all the sources of information, which they can control through propaganda (see Political Terms), they can fool the public into believing and trusting them. Any opponents are ruthlessly eliminated in as bloody and public a way as possible to frighten the public into obeying them. In this way they become corrupt, vicious tyrants.

EDUCATION AND LEARNING

There is a proverbial (see Literary Terms) saying that 'knowledge is power'. The pigs are clearly the most intelligent animals on the farm and soon take control of the running of the farm. They are able to do so as they have taught themselves to read and write. Initially they support the revolution by spreading it to the other animals. As most of the farm animals cannot remember Major's speech and his ideas clearly, the pigs simplify them into seven slogans or commandments. Snowball tries to teach the other animals to read and write. Increasingly however, the pigs take advantage of them instead of actually leading and helping the creatures. The gulf between the ideal of the revolution, what the pigs pretend they are doing and the reality of the situation becomes increasingly widened. The role of education is an important one. The pigs are eventually able to dominate the animals. The pigs acquire much of their learning as they can read and with the knowledge they acquire, are able to achieve and hold power over the other animals. Snowball is able to prepare for Jones's attack as he has read a book of Caesar's campaigns and is full of ideas for 'innovations and improvements' (p. 30) that he has learnt from reading copies of the *Farmer and Stockbreeder*.

What does this suggest about the pigs' view of education?

Orwell presents two contrasting views of education. Snowball seeks to educate all the animals whilst Napoleon is seen to concentrate his efforts on a smaller group when he nurtures the puppies. Rather than expose them to the wider group, they are kept in isolation and given their own instruction. It becomes clear that this is not education but rather indoctrination (see Political Terms). In a similar way, young pigs will also be educated later in the novel away from the rest of the animals. Napoleon is also able to use his learning to make life more enjoyable. The pigs discover how to brew alcohol and appear to enjoy the results.

Snowball's attempts to educate the animals are laudable but to some extent are doomed. Mollie uses her knowledge of the alphabet to pursue her own vanity,

Benjamin simply refuses to read and the more intelligent animals (such as the dogs) will not extend their knowledge. This is possibly summed up by the fact that Muriel reads from a rubbish tip, giving some idea of what Orwell thinks about the uses to which the animals put their reading. Few of them are willing to broaden their horizons and this makes them vulnerable.

How would the course of the revolution alter if the animals were keen to, or indeed able to, learn? What do you think Orwell is saying about the role of education in society?

Boxer and Clover are willing to read but lack the intelligence to do so. However well-meaning or kind they are, their lack of appreciation of what is actually going on around them means that they do not see the way in which they are being used by the pigs. Both a lack of intelligence and literacy are seen as leaving the animals in a vulnerable position later. In addition, Snowball's aims are in some ways ridiculous, his list detailing their reading fails to address the complacency of some of the animals and their differing levels of ability. It serves little purpose.

The pigs are able to exploit the other animals as they are intelligent enough to manipulate the truth in such a way that their evil actions seem perfectly acceptable. This is achieved through a skilful use of language.

LANGUAGE & POWER

Orwell was concerned about the relationship between language and power. In his essay *Literature and Totalitarianism,* Orwell stated that 'totalitarianism has abolished freedom of thought to an extent unheard of in any previous age'. He believed that this was achieved not only by preventing or forbidding certain thoughts or ideas but by telling people exactly what to think. In this way, the totalitarian state doesn't just control one's actions and movements but one's thoughts as well. This is achieved through propaganda.

This idea was developed by Orwell in his novel 1984.

We see this from the beginning of the novel when Snowball simplifies Major's ideas into slogans, in an

Look carefully at the uses to which these slogans are put in the story.

effort to make the less intelligent animals understand the principles of Animalism. For example, Major's statement that 'Whatever goes upon four legs is a friend. Whatever goes upon two legs is an enemy' is reduced to the slogan 'Four legs good. Two legs bad'. This simplification can lead to a loss of meaning and become dangerous as we see when the sheep use the chant to drown any opposition to Napoleon in the meetings.

Propaganda (see Political Terms) is a method of convincing others of the truth of your arguments. The propagandist is clearly presented in this book by the figure of Squealer. We can agree with Orwell that he turns black into white – we see him do it. He invents questionable scientific evidence to convince the animals that the pigs should have the apples, reads out lists of statistics that have been forged and tells them of written evidence (which he never produces) to prove that Snowball is in league with Jones, knowing very well that the animals cannot read.

Find additional quotes to support these points in Squealer's speeches throughout the novel.

The propagandist uses several weapons. A selective use of the truth is apparent when Squealer tells the other animals that milk is good for the pigs in Chapter 3. So it is, but it is also good for other animals on the farm such as the hens. He also uses rhetorical questions (see Literary Terms) which do not require an answer from the audience – so the speaker does the thinking for them, 'Surely, comrades, you do not want Jones back?' (p. 35). This quote also demonstrates a further technique: that of pin-pointing the enemy. In doing this, the audience will forget their problems and concentrate on the enemy outside their society. The pigs constantly remind the animals that without their protection, the unthinkable would happen: Jones would come back. This in itself is often enough to silence the creatures.

The use of language was important to Orwell as he felt that sloppy language made it easier to have 'foolish thoughts'. This was worrying, as in this way, outrageous ideas could be presented in such a way that they seemed acceptable. Language is used to disguise the real meaning of a word. In *Animal Farm* we see several examples of this, from Squealer's use of the word 'readjustment' to tell the animals that their rations are being reduced, to the final perversion of the word 'equality'. The slogan 'All Animals Are Equal But Some Are More Equal Than Others' (p. 83) is nonsense but disguises the lack of equality on the farm.

The way in which we use language is important as it can change the way we think.

Some people argue that this is not just a feature of totalitarian governments. One British government spokesman denied an accusation that he had lied, saying that he had only been 'economical with the truth'. Orwell's warnings about the ways in which words and their meanings can be twisted are still relevant today.

STRUCTURE

Animal Farm follows a conventional narrative structure. Its events are told in chronological order by the narrator. The story itself contains a believable mixture of human and animal characters – even when the human characters are seen to clearly understand what the animals are saying – for example, when Pilkington makes his speech to Napoleon at the end of the novel, the reader believes that the two understand each other.

The story is divided into ten chapters which trace the decline of the high ideals of the Animalist revolution. The book is also structured in a more subtle way. Once the revolution has happened, several chapters open by referring to the suffering of the animals or the harsh winters (Chapters 5, 6 and 7 all open in this way) and end with the gradual perversion of one of the

Commandments. These remind the readers of the gradual destruction of Major's ideals. Once Boxer has been taken to his death at the close of Chapter 9, the pace of the story rapidly increases. In Chapter 10, the pigs are seen walking and the barn wall is repainted and the remainder of the Commandments are broken within two pages. It is as though the murder of Napoleon's most loyal worker speeds the pigs' descent into evil.

The repetition of various ideas and images forms a pattern in the text and links events together. In particular Major's speech at the start of the novel is echoed and referred to throughout the novel, to provide a standard by which the pigs' actions are judged. The placing of the speech at the start of the novel, means that the reader shares the animals' enthusiasm for the vision of the future and becomes progressively more disappointed as the novel continues and we see those ideals destroyed: we are told several times that the animals work like 'slaves'. The repetition of 'Beasts of England' at the end of Chapter 7 shows its decline from a song with a hopeful vision of the future to a subversive and illegal anthem. The recurrent appearance of the menacing dogs also ensures that the reader never forgets the terror and violence that underpins Napoleon's rule: the sheep's mindless and repetitive bleating is used in a similar way. Each time one of these elements is reintroduced into the novel a further point about the destruction of the revolution is made.

In a similar way, the repeated breaking of the Commandments and the animals' continual checking of the wall, makes clear to the reader, the gradual distortion of Major's ideals until we reach the shocking climax, in which all pretence of following the Commandments is abandoned by the pigs, in favour of open terror and oppression, signified by the whips.

Look at Major's speech. Go through the novel again and find exactly where each one of his ideals is destroyed.

The structure of *Animal Farm* helps to clarify the theme
of the betrayed revolution by showing the reader in
several stages, through the repetition of certain key
images and phrases, how the pigs pervert Major's rules.

CHARACTERS

NAPOLEON

Tyrant
Cunning
Ruthless
Vain
Hypocrite
Aloof
Stalin

Napoleon was the name of a revolutionary who ended
up gaining power and tyrannising (see Political Terms)
the French people. From simply one of several pigs at
the start of the novel, Napoleon becomes the most
dominant animal on the farm, widening the gap
between himself and the others by a gradual
accumulation of power. He, more than anyone else, is
responsible for the betrayal of Major's dream.

In Chapter 2, Napoleon is immediately linked with
Snowball. The latter appears to be one of the most
engaging characters in terms of his plans and ideals and
seems to put Napoleon in the shade. In contrast to the
more talkative Snowball, Napoleon is relatively silent.
However, he still gets his own way, suggesting a
determined character. Napoleon and Snowball have
differing ideas about Animalism. Their disagreements
parallel those of Stalin and Trotsky (see Theme on The
Russian Revolution). Napoleon's devious nature is clear
from the end of the second chapter in which he places
himself in charge of the milk which will later be
commandeered for the pigs' use. He takes control of the
food supply quickly. His taking away of the puppies
shows how his strike for power is premeditated. His
expulsion of Snowball demonstrates for the first time
the extent of his power – Napoleon appears to have
gained the support of the dogs and sheep and is helped
by the fickle nature of the crowd.

From the start it seems, Napoleon turns events to his
own advantage. In Chapter 4, when the farm is

attacked in the 'Battle of the Cowshed', Napoleon is
nowhere to be seen. Cowardice is hinted at and his
readiness to rewrite history later in the novel shows the
ways in which Napoleon is prepared to twist the truth
for his own ends.

The Seven Commandments are perverted throughout
the novel to suit his aims. He announces his intentions
to the animals who are terrified into silent agreement,
when it is clear – as when Napoleon decides to engage
in trade – that the plans have already been made. That
Napoleon needs the animals to be pacified is apparent
through the use he makes of Squealer. Whenever the
pigs infringe one of Major's commandments, Squealer
is sent to convince the other animals that that is the
correct interpretation. Napoleon secures his rule
through an unpleasant mix of lies, distortion and
hypocrisy.

*Look at the way
in which
Napoleon's actions
are distorted by
Squealer later in
the novel.*

Napoleon becomes increasingly self-seeking as the
novel progresses. The reader is aware that the
commandment about the equality of the animals has
been broken long before it is altered on the wall of the
farm. Napoleon's increasing preoccupation with his
position and status demonstrates the way that he uses
the revolution for his own personal gain. He keeps
himself remote from the other animals, lives in luxury
(he dines from Crown Derby china and eats sugar) and
stages elaborate ceremonies in his own honour.

Napoleon ensures that Snowball is blamed for any of
his own failings and creates an atmosphere of hysteria
in which animals will confess to the most ludicrous
crimes. In making use of this Napoleon demonstrates
the bloody nature of his rule and its descent into
tyranny. His power is absolute and the uses to which he
puts it are terrifying. The extent of his cruelty is
apparent in his treatment of Boxer.

Once he has gained power, it is clear that it erodes any

original belief he had in Animalism. He systematically destroys all of Major's tenets as he gradually adopts the behaviour and vices of the humans that Major so viciously attacked. He is the archetypal dictator (see Political Terms).

SQUEALER

Articulate
Plausible
Hypocritical
Propagandist

One of the most significant characters is the pig Squealer. We are told that he can 'turn black into white' (p. 9). He plausibly defends the pigs' actions in brilliant pieces of rhetoric (see Literary Terms) which are often underlined by the basic threat of Jones's return. The animals then are given little option but to accede to the pigs' actions. Squealer's 'shrill voice', 'twinkling eyes' and his mannerisms emphasise the persuasiveness of this character. He is like the modern spin-doctor, presenting events and ideas in the form that best suits his leader's ideas. He is crucial to Napoleon's success. Squealer is responsible for the devious alterations of the Commandments which are amended each time one is broken, to reflect the reality of life under the pigs. He presents each flouting of the rules as a perfectly reasonable action and is able to confuse and persuade the animals in such a way as to eliminate opposition. He gives the animals meaningless lists of statistics in an attempt to convince them that life under Napoleon is getting better. He works solely for Napoleon and clearly benefits from his patronage – he grows increasingly fat as the novel progresses.

That Squealer does not rely on his eloquence alone is apparent from the references to the dogs that accompany him around the farm. An element of cowardice in his character is also suggested in Chapter 8, when he is 'unaccountably absent' (p. 65) from the fighting.

The sinister side to his character is apparent when he is seen noting the signs of resistance to Napoleon – even when these arrive in the form of gentle questions from characters such as Boxer. His ugly sideways looks and the subsequent attack on Boxer suggest that Squealer's propaganda (see Political Terms) is more sinister than simply ensuring that the animals obey Napoleon: it is also used to eliminate anyone who doubts him. Squealer's arrogance and contempt for the other animals shows the dismissive attitude that the propagandist has towards those he exploits.

SNOWBALL

Articulate
Innovative
Brilliant
strategist
Moderniser
Idealist
Trotsky

What do you think the farm would be like if Snowball was in charge?

Snowball's character is that of an intellectual. The pig is described in the opening of Chapter 2 as brilliant and inventive. However he is also criticised as being superficial.

He energetically promotes the revolution, censuring Mollie for her desire for ribbons. He organises the animals into several committees, teaching the animals several skills, the most important of which are reading and writing.

He appears then to care for the wellbeing of the other animals – although he endorses Napoleon's seizure of the apples in Chapter 3. He also dismisses the killing of humans when he says to Boxer 'The only good human being is a dead one' (p. 27). His unsentimentality suggests a coldness on his part which, whilst not as extreme as Napoleon's, at least makes the reader wonder how much better the revolution would have been under him.

Snowball is brave in battle and a brilliant strategist. He inspires others to make similar sacrifices in the 'Battle of the Cowshed', which was for Snowball a moment of glory.

Yet for all his brilliance, Snowball fails to secure power. He fails to notice Napoleon's steady climb to power – or the use he makes of the dogs. Terror and force mean

that Napoleon can control the animals in a way that
Snowball's eloquence never can. He is defeated and
nearly killed just as it seems to the reader that he has
convinced the animals of the wisdom of his ideas.

After his expulsion he, like Mr Jones (with whom he is
later said to have collaborated), becomes a mythical
figure, a scapegoat on whom every misdemeanour,
however trivial, is blamed. Any animal linked to him is
immediately executed whether they are guilty or not.
His place in the farm's history becomes completely
distorted and his contribution to the revolution denied.

He is presented as an idealist who is unaware of the
calculating and ruthless natures of those around him.

MAJOR

*Oldest animal on
farm*
Kindly
Statesmanlike
Wise
Marxist thinking
*Suggests
revolution*

Major is seen as a kindly pig who is a natural leader. He
is the oldest animal on the farm and thus is seen to
have acquired much wisdom. Once he has died it
appears that there is little control over the course that
the revolution will take.

Major's speech is a mix of Marxism and Leninism. It
establishes the theoretical basis of the novel: the
struggle for freedom and against tyranny for a society of
equals. His political ideas are explained subtly as he
suggests a utopian vision of a society in which cruelty
and suffering are distant memories. In this way complex
political ideas are presented in a readable form.

*Look at the devices
Major uses to
convince his
audience that what
he is saying is true.*

His ideas are essentially those of communism which
formed the basis of government by Lenin in Russia
during the 1920s. As the pigs develop these ideas and
then pervert them, so Stalin took Lenin's doctrines and
twisted them for his own benefit.

Throughout the novel, his memory serves as the beacon
of the original aims of the revolution and it is when
Napoleon states that the marching past of Major's skull
will no longer take place that we realise the big

Y

difference between Major's aims and those of
Napoleon.

Kind
Trusting
Loyal
Hardworking
Proletariat

From the opening of the novel, we see how kind and
gentle the cart-horses Boxer and Clover are towards the
other animals. Boxer is a loyal follower of the revolution
and is prepared to make sacrifices for it. His selflessness
and dedication are perhaps most strongly apparent
when after Snowball's speech against ribbons, he gives
up the hat he uses to protect him from flies. Much of
the success of the harvest depends on Boxer's strength
and total commitment. He is determined to work for
the farm – in contrast to Mollie and the cat. Boxer and
Clover represent the proletariat (see Political Terms),
Boxer's strength reminding us of the Soviet worker
Alexander Stakhanov who set superhuman targets for
other Soviet workers.

Despite his loyalty and dedication to the revolution,
Boxer's compassion and humility are apparent. He is
devastated when he thinks he has killed the stable lad
in Chapter 4 and makes it clear that he does not want
to kill even his most fervent enemy. Sadly, this view is
not shared by the pigs.

Boxer is a loyal and dedicated follower of an ideal that
he does not fully understand. His lack of intelligence
and unquestioning trust in the pigs mean that he is
vulnerable to their exploitation. He is gullible and easily
manipulated. This does not merely result in him
suffering under the pigs. According to Orwell, such
behaviour is literally fatal.

His integrity and honesty are shown by his defence of
Snowball, which is noted by Squealer. It is only his
strength that saves him from the dogs when they attack
him in Chapter 7. That Napoleon is prepared to
destroy him at the meeting is a horrifying symbol of
how corrupt the pigs have become.

Boxer's blind faith in the pigs is seen as disastrous. Confronted with the horrifying massacre of the animals on the farm, Boxer (who is clearly upset by what he has seen) blames himself and buries himself in his work. His constant self-sacrificing is clear in his defence of the farm and his insistence on working until he sees the windmill rebuilt – even though this will cost him his life. That his murder is postponed rather than prevented is clear when he is taken off in the knacker's van. The pigs' callous disregard for the one figure without whom their success would not be possible is chilling. The fact that those who do see through the pigs' actions warn Boxer too late, emphasises Orwell's pessimistic predictions for those in society who have a blind trust in their rulers. The final insult is the pigs' banquet at which they toast his honour with whisky – which has been bought by the proceeds of his death. Even in death Boxer is used to the pigs' advantage.

CLOVER

Kind
Protective
Loyal
Caring
Proletariat

One of the most attractive figures in the novel, she is a 'stout motherly mare' who has had four foals. She is the one constant character in the novel and indeed a unique one. She is the only character whose thoughts we are allowed to see (at the end of Chapter 7). By the end of the novel, she is exhausted and overworked – at the age of fourteen, with her rheumy eyes, she still works as hard as at the start of the novel. She is not as strong as Boxer, but she is slightly brighter.

She is seen as continually kind and protective – at the opening of the novel she shelters the ducklings. In the same way, after the executions, she comforts the animals as they retreat to the Knoll. She cares tenderly for Boxer when he splits his hoof and pleads with him not to overwork himself. Clover demonstrates the kindness and tenderness that is destroyed by the pigs.

Like Boxer, she is a loyal disciple of the Animalist

revolution. She criticises Mollie for her betrayal of the animals' work.

Clover's limited intelligence and her reluctance to confront her doubts prevent her from rebelling or challenging the pigs' rule, even though she sees the horrors of the farm around her. We suspect that of all the animals (bar Benjamin) she alone has some inkling of what is taking place – she continually checks the commandments as a result of her doubts, but never acts upon them.

She remains loyal to Napoleon and, as an indication of the unquestioning nature of this loyalty, we are told this immediately after the executions and after her unconscious feelings are revealed. We feel frustrated and horrified that even after such events the animals still acquiesce to the pigs – showing the pigs' total dominance of the farm animals and how much this depends on the farm animals' own timidity and loyalty.

Clover's loyalty to the principle of Animalism is clear at the end of the novel. Again, she is a significant character for the reader – as we see the final scene through her eyes. This is the way that we see the changing faces of the men and the pigs and see the pigs' final descent into evil. The fact that this is witnessed by an uncomprehending and horrified member of the farm, who is unable to understand the extent to which the animals have been exploited by the pigs, makes the scene all the more effective.

BENJAMIN

Cynical
Intelligent
Loyal to Boxer
and Clover

Benjamin the donkey is seen as a cynic. The novel deals with the way in which power is seen to corrupt and traces the descent of the revolution from its idealistic start to its tragic conclusion. Benjamin, unlike the other animals, questions whether the animals really will be better off as the result of the revolution. However, he is not uncaring as his relationship with Clover, and especially Boxer, later shows. His cynicism remains unchanged in the light of the success of the harvest. At the 'Battle of the Cowshed' he is in the thick of the fighting, which questions how critical he is of the regime at the farm.

Benjamin is in some ways one of the most interesting characters in the book. He is loyal to the horses but repeatedly refuses to read the commandments – believing that it will create trouble. He appears to be aware of the true nature of the revolution throughout the novel but refuses to interfere when he sees the pigs doing wrong. It is only when his best friend is being led to his death that he alerts the others – but by that stage it is too late to help Boxer. He is the one who reads out the final betrayal of the animals and is with Clover when the true extent of the betrayal at the farmhouse is revealed.

MR JONES

Owner of Manor Farm

Incapable

Drunk

Self-indulgent

Cruel

Tsar

Capitalist

From the start of the novel, Mr Jones is seen as an unfit manager of the farm. The story opens with him being incapable of shutting up the hen coop as he is drunk. He is a 'hard master' (p. 11) and is cruel and lazy. After the revolution, he spends most of his time whingeing in the pub. His attempt to regain the farm ends in humiliation when he lands in the manure heap. His fellow farmers fail to help him and he ends up dying in a home for drunks, a pathetic character. Jones represents the Tsar and the corrupt regime that the revolution replaces.

His cruelty is stressed by Major in his speech and the thoughtless nature of his violence is apparent in his random shooting to quell the noise from the barn. However, Jones's presence in the book outweighs his real appearance – the pigs continually use his name to intimidate the farm animals into doing their bidding. This eventually leads to the almost mythic status he has in the novel.

MOLLIE

Vain
Frivolous
Parasite
White Russians

Mollie 'the foolish, pretty white mare' (p. 2), represents the White Russians, who under the Tsar had a privileged life. She is reluctant to lose these privileges and is not committed to the revolution. She has not suffered in the way Major describes the suffering of the other animals. She does not share the other animals belief in the benefits of the revolution and certainly doesn't work as hard as they do for it. She seems fascinated and envious of the luxuries acquired by the humans and hankers after them. Mollie and the cat can best be described as parasites. They contribute little to life on the farm and appear to be only interested in what they can use for their own advantage.

Mollie leaves the farm as soon as life there appears to become more demanding. She is incapable of making any sacrifice (such as giving up her ribbons) unlike Boxer. Such selfishness is perhaps one reason why the revolution fails. However, as life on the farm deteriorates for the other animals, the reader is left wondering just how foolish her departure was.

MOSES

Deceitful
Articulate
Russian
Orthodox Church

As the religious connotations of his name suggests, Moses the raven represents the Russian Orthodox Church. He is never to be trusted (he is described on p. 10 as a spy) as he convinces many of the animals that there is a life after their present one. In this way the animals would accept their sufferings as a temporary trial to be endured before they find eternal peace and happiness. This is doubly wrong in Orwell's eyes as the animals are fooling themselves. It is their own unquestioning belief that condemns them.

At the start, Moses is seen to be the human's pet – in the same way that the Russian Orthodox Church supported the Tsar. Moses's return after several years and his acceptance by the pigs parallels the attempts by Stalin to gain acceptance for his cruel actions in Poland from the Catholic church. This was greeted with derision abroad.

The dogs

From the start of the novel, the dogs are seen as loyal animals. They are closely linked to the pigs; when Major calls the meeting at the barn they enter with them. Later we are told that they wag their tails to Napoleon in the same way that they did to Jones, emphasising the similarity between their two masters.

During Major's speech the dogs chase the rats into their holes and are prevented by Major from harming them as he says it is contrary to the rules of Animalism. However, throughout the book they become the force which Napoleon uses to suppress any potential opposition. They are closely linked to him: we see that he has preplanned the role that they will occupy in his society. They are the counterpart of Stalin's secret police.

Along with the pigs, the dogs are privileged and lead more comfortable lives than the other animals. This is the dogs' reward for ruthlessly dealing with any objectors and murdering any opposition.

The sheep

The sheep represent the most stupid elements of society. Their understanding of the aims of the revolution is limited to bleating out the slogan 'Four legs good, two legs bad', and when Squealer decides to alter this it takes him a week to get them to learn the amended version. The damage that such mindless support can do is apparent from the Sunday meetings, when they drown out Snowball's speech. They become unknowing tools of oppression as each time a potential moment of protest comes up, their bleating prevents anyone else being heard. In this way they stifle any chances of free speech on the farm.

The hens

The only group that attempt to show any resistance to Napoleon are the hens. In his speech, Major specifically criticised the taking of hens' eggs and demands that this inhumane practice be stopped, yet under Napoleon, the hens are expected to do just that. They retaliate by smashing their eggs, in the same way that the kulaks destroyed their own farms rather than let Stalin's government take them over. Napoleon's ruthless suppression of the hens demonstrates his willingness to use terror and murder to achieve his own ends, in the same way that Stalin executed and exiled those peasants who opposed him.

The pigs

From the start of the novel the pigs are seen, in general, as the most intelligent and capable creatures. As a group, they understand Animalism and translate it into easy slogans for the other animals. They quickly become the decision-makers in the farm. To some extent then, equality of any kind seems unlikely especially as the pigs are so easily able to manipulate an ignorant crowd. They become a second aristocracy in the novel, exploiting the animals and living a life of luxury that is unimaginable to the rest of the farm animals.

The cat

We hear very little of the cat once Napoleon is in power. She appears to represent the forces of self-interest and hypocrisy – as we see when she attempts to persuade the sparrows to read. She has as little to do with the revolution as possible but is willing to enjoy its benefits.

Pilkington

A farmer, like Jones, Pilkington in the allegory (see Literary Terms) stands for Britain under Churchill. He, like Napoleon, is keen to exploit his own workers. Pilkington is not a model farmer, Foxwood Farm is described as overgrown and neglected, whilst its owner enjoys himself hunting. In this respect, he is presented as a gentleman farmer. Napoleon tried to play Pilkington off against Frederick by persuading him to help, but when Frederick attacks the farm, Pilkington refuses to help.

By the end of the novel, the farmer and the pigs are
seen as allies – albeit temporarily. In the same way,
Stalin and Churchill were allied at the Tehran
conference with Roosevelt. That this trust is only a
façade is apparent in the allegations of cheating
which close the novel – as the Cold War reflected a
rapid deterioration in the relationships between
Russia and the Western powers after the Second World
War.

Frederick   No more likeable than Pilkington, his farm is at least
better run. He is a hard businessman and argumentative
but shrewd.

The striking characterisation is that of his cruelty. This
appears to refer to Hitler who treated Jews with
horrifying cruelty.

Napoleon's efforts to trade with and bargain with
Frederick are seen as a misguided attempt at business as
Frederick tricks him. In a similar way, Hitler and
Stalin's non-aggression pact was completely ignored
by Hitler when he invaded Russia. This invasion
was a violent and destructive one, in the same way as
the attack on the windmill is seen as a demolition of all
that the animals have achieved.

Mrs Jones   Very little is seen of her in the book but when she is
mentioned it is in an unfavourable light – she is either
snoring or running away from the farm.

Whymper   The solicitor is seen to profit from the animals' misery
and suffering – as the result of his dealing with Animal
Farm he can buy himself a dogcart. He is described as
'a sly-looking little man' (p. 40).

Other humans   The man who becomes Mollie's owner is described
as 'a fat, red-faced man in check breeches and gaiters'
(p. 29) whilst the man who drives Boxer to his death
is also described as 'a sly-looking man in a low-crowned
bowler hat' (p. 75). The repeated reference to the

slyness of the human characters emphasises their unpleasantness and untrustworthiness.

None of the humans in *Animal Farm* are presented in an attractive light. However horrifying the result of Napoleon's rule, Orwell seems to suggest that the animals were right to rebel against Jones's cruelty.

LANGUAGE & STYLE

Orwell's style is so 'transparent' and simple that it is hard to realise that the reader's views of events in the novel and the characters are being carefully directed.

His style is straightforward and direct and we tend to take what he says at face value. We do not question his interpretation of the characters and feel that he is telling the truth. This is problematic in a novel which is itself about the way in which power distorts language. We trust the writer.

Orwell called the novel a fairy story and this is suggested in the simplicity of its style. Along with its use of a farmyard setting and animal characters it seems to be a perfect book for children. However, upon reading, it is clear that this is not the case at all. The ending of the novel is particularly bleak. No solution is held out. It is clear that there is no possible happy ending. The effect of the work comes from the author's use of the discrepancy between what we anticipate the novel will be about – a cute story of everyday farm animals; and its real subject – the bloody and cruel way in which the animals' hopes of a happy and free future are destroyed.

Orwell and the English language

Orwell thought that, to a large extent, language created meaning – 'one ought to recognise that the present political chaos is connected with the decay of language, and that one can probably bring about some improvement by starting at the verbal end'. In *Animal Farm* it is clear in which ways language is used by the pigs to distort the truth. In *1984*, his later novel, there is an official language, 'Newspeak', which is used by those in power to enforce particular ways of thinking.

Orwell established certain rules for writers to follow – these were in an effort to avoid clichéd, and thus mindless, language and to make the reader think about what they were reading. He suggested that writers simplify their words, use straightforward language rather than foreign or technical words which could mislead the reader and fail to make the meaning clear. This was especially true of political writing. Language had to try, as far as possible, to reflect the truth of an issue rather than be distorted or relay false sentiments or feelings. In *Animal Farm*, language is used to cover up meaning. We see the pigs make use of the word 'equality' to mean its opposite.

Try to find examples of irony at the start of Chapter 6. Consider to what effect they are used.

The novel is a satire (see Literary Terms). As a result Orwell uses irony (see Literary Terms) to communicate his feelings and thoughts to the reader. This is an important feature of his style (see Context and Setting).

Little figurative language (see Literary Terms) is used in the novel. Its symbols are, on the whole, obvious – as one would probably expect in an allegory (see Literary Terms). The instances in which the writing does become more descriptive are when the animals look at their farm during the harvest after the revolution and after the execution (Chapters 2 and 7). Even so, the writing here is still strictly controlled and simple; in Chapter 2 the animals lick up 'clods of the black earth and snuffed its rich scent' (p. 13). Orwell never lets you lose sight of his purpose – to convince the reader of the value of the ideals for which the farm animals had revolted.

PART FOUR

Study skills

How to use quotations

One of the secrets of success in writing essays is the way you use quotations. There are five basic principles:

- Put inverted commas at the beginning and end of the quotation
- Write the quotation exactly as it appears in the original
- Do not use a quotation that repeats what you have just written
- Use the quotation so that it fits into your sentence
- Keep the quotation as short as possible

Quotations should be used to develop the line of thought in your essays.

Your comment should not duplicate what is in your quotation. For example:

The meeting begins with the sound of the dogs barking outside the barn, 'there was a terrible baying sound outside'.

Far more effective is to write:

The meeting begins with 'a terrible baying sound outside'.

However, the most sophisticated way of using the writer's words is to embed them into your sentence:

When the dogs taste blood they appear to go 'quite mad'.

When you use quotations in this way, you are demonstrating the ability to use text as evidence to support your ideas - not simply including words from the original to prove you have read it.

Everyone writes differently. Work through the suggestions given here and adapt the advice to suit your own style and interests. This will improve your essay-writing skills and allow your personal voice to emerge.

The following points indicate in ascending order the skills of essay writing:

- Picking out one or two facts about the story and adding the odd detail
- Writing about the text by retelling the story
- Retelling the story and adding a quotation here and there
- Organising an answer which explains what is happening in the text and giving quotations to support what you write

....

- Writing in such a way as to show that you have thought about the intentions of the writer of the text and that you understand the techniques used
- Writing at some length, giving your viewpoint on the text and commenting by picking out details to support your views
- Looking at the text as a work of art, demonstrating clear critical judgement and explaining to the reader of your essay how the enjoyment of the text is assisted by literary devices, linguistic effects and psychological insights; showing how the text relates to the time when it was written

The dotted line above represents the division between lower and higher level grades. Higher-level performance begins when you start to consider your response as a reader of the text. The highest level is reached when you offer an enthusiastic personal response and show how this piece of literature is a product of its time.

Coursework Set aside an hour or so at the start of your work to plan
essay what you have to do.

- List all the points you feel are needed to cover the task. Collect page references of information and quotations that will support what you have to say. A helpful tool is the highlighter pen: this saves painstaking copying and enables you to target precisely what you want to use.
- Focus on what you consider to be the main points of the essay. Try to sum up your argument in a single sentence, which could be the closing sentence of your essay. Depending on the essay title, it could be a statement about a character: Napoleon's rise to power from the start of the novel is carefully planned; an opinion about setting: Orwell's use of a farm as the book's setting provides a clear allegorical (see Literary Terms) framework for the novel; or a judgement on a theme: throughout the novel it is clear that power corrupts.
- Make a short essay plan. Use the first paragraph to introduce the argument you wish to make. In the following paragraphs develop this argument with details, examples and other possible points of view. Sum up your argument in the last paragraph. Check you have answered the question.
- Write the essay, remembering all the time the central point you are making.
- On completion, go back over what you have written to eliminate careless errors and improve expression. Read it aloud to yourself, or, if you are feeling more confident, to a relative or friend.

If you can, try to type your essay using a word processor. This will allow you to correct and improve your writing without spoiling its appearance.

Examination essay

The essay written in an examination often carries more marks than the coursework essay even though it is written under considerable time pressure.

In the revision period build up notes on various aspects of the text you are using. Fortunately, in acquiring this set of York Notes on *Animal Farm*, you have made a prudent beginning! York Notes are set out to give you vital information and help you to construct your personal overview of the text.

Make notes with appropriate quotations about the key issues of the set text. Go into the examination knowing your text and having a clear set of opinions about it.

In most English Literature examinations you can take in copies of your set books. This in an enormous advantage although it may lull you into a false sense of security. Beware! There is simply not enough time in an examination to read the book from scratch.

In the examination

- Read the question paper carefully and remind yourself what you have to do.
- Look at the questions on your set texts to select the one that most interests you and mentally work out the points you wish to stress.
- Remind yourself of the time available and how you are going to use it.
- Briefly map out a short plan in note form that will keep your writing on track and illustrate the key argument you want to make.
- Then set about writing it.
- When you have finished, check through to eliminate errors.

To summarise: these are the keys to success

- **Know the text**
- **Have a clear understanding of and opinions on the storyline, characters, setting, themes and writer's concerns**
- **Select the right material**
- **Plan and write a clear response, continually bearing the question in mind**

A typical essay question on *Animal Farm* is followed by a sample essay plan in note form. This does not present the only answer to the question, merely one answer. Do not be afraid to include your own ideas, and leave out some of those in the sample! Remember that quotations are essential to prove and illustrate the points you make.

Discuss the significance of the Seven Commandments in *Animal Farm*.

Part 1
Introduction

- *Animal Farm* is an allegory (see Literary Terms). Explain the term.
- It is an analysis of the events following the Russian Revolution. Therefore the nature of the Commandments have a deeper significance.

Part 2
The Command-
ments

- Association of name with Christianity's Ten Commandments. Unalterable and holy law suggested.
- Established for all animals to understand the principles of the revolution. For this reason written on wall.
- Elaborate on the gradual distortion of the rules by Napoleon and the excuses Squealer makes to justify them.
- Alterations appear mysteriously on the wall. Why?
- The gradual distortion of the Commandments by the pigs is one way in which the author makes the reader aware of the progressive shift away from Major's original ideals into Napoleon's dictatorship.

Part 3
Conclusion

- Recap briefly on your points regarding *Animal Farm* as an allegory.
- Outline simply what light this sheds on Russian history.
- Outline what the Commandments reveal about the way the revolution has been altered since Major died and how Napoleon now rules the farm.

- Mention Orwell's purpose, which was to draw attention to the corruption of Stalin's government.
- Briefly discuss his style – written in clear, simple language.

In such an essay you must ensure that you answer the question. Do not go into extensive detail regarding Russian history but focus instead on the book.

FURTHER QUESTIONS

Make a plan as shown above and attempt these questions.

1 What is a satire (see Literary Terms)? With reference to *Animal Farm*, identify the targets that Orwell attacks. Is he successful?
2 Look at two main characters in the novel. How does their relationship alter as the novel progresses?
3 How are certain words or phrases altered in *Animal Farm*. Who changes them? What does this tell you about Orwell's own ideas about language?
4 *Animal Farm* is subtitled 'A Fairy Story'. How suitable is this description of the novel?

PART FIVE

CULTURAL CONNECTIONS

BROADER PERSPECTIVES

Here are some suggestions of other works which put
Animal Farm in a wider context. The following books
and film should give you plenty to think about!

Books   George Orwell's *1984* (O.U.P., 1984 – first published
1949) provides an obvious point of comparison with
Animal Farm – especially in the methods used by Big
Brother to control the people. It is very useful to
compare the two books in terms of their use of
propaganda (see Political Terms).

George Orwell's *The Collected Essays, Journalism and
Letters*, which is in four volumes and is edited by Sonia
Orwell and Ian Angus (Penguin, 1970 – first published
1958), is an interesting and readable collection. It
includes Orwell's essays on the use of language.

Aldous Huxley's novel *Brave New World* (Longman,
1985) also deals with the creation of a new society and
is an interesting contrast to *Animal Farm*.

Films   A cartoon version of *Animal Farm* was produced in the
1950s. It is particularly useful as it alters the ending of
the novel completely. See which ending you prefer – or
which one you think Orwell would have been happier
with.

There are plenty of anthropomorphic (see Literary
Terms) characters in the film *Babe* (1995). Again, it is
interesting to compare the film's use of the farmyard
setting and the characterisation of the various animals.

allegory a story or piece of writing that contains two coherent meanings. *Animal Farm* is therefore a political allegory because both levels of meaning, that of the lives of the animals on the farm and the deeper references to the Russian Revolution, make sense.

anthropomorphic this term describes animals who are seen to behave like humans. They talk and think for example.

fable a fable is a short story which contains a moral. Fables make use of anthropomorphic characters. One writer, Aesop, was famous for these works.

figurative language any form of language that contains more than the bare facts and is used to create effect e.g. her head was spinning.

genre genre is a term for a type or kind of literature. For example, an example of the gothic genre would be *Dracula*.

irony when writers use words that suggest the opposite of what they normally mean, we say that they are being ironic. An example of this in *Animal Farm* occurs when Orwell describes Squealer 'who had unaccountably been absent' (p. 65) from the 'Battle of the Windmill'. The reader knows that he was not unaccountably absent but had probably been hiding to avoid injury.

maxim a short and effective statement which suggests ideal ways of behaving.

motto a short phrase containing a simple statement or idea.

pseudonym a book published under a name other than the author's. Another example of a pen-name is that of George Eliot whose real name was Mary Ann Evans.

proverb a short saying which deals with a generally accepted truth: for example 'Too many cooks spoil the broth'.

rhetoric the art of speaking (and writing) effectively so as to persuade an audience.

rhetorical question a question that does not require an answer but is used to emphasise a particular point.

satire literature which targets an issue, institution or idea and attacks it in such a way as to make it look ridiculous or worthy of contempt. It is not the same as simply making fun of something, as the satirical writer has a purpose in attacking the target, other than making people laugh.

third person narrative a story that is told about people or events (using 'he', 'she', or 'they') by a narrator who does not write 'I', but appears as an unseen narrator of events.

Political terms

capitalist according to Karl Marx, a capitalist is someone who has money and invests it in a business. They then make a profit if the business does well.

dictator a ruler whose decisions do not need anyone else's agreement. Often, in dictatorships, any form of opposition has been abolished, leaving the ruler with absolute power.

indoctrination to brainwash someone into believing a particular opinion.

kulak a land-owning peasant. After the Russian Revolution, they did not want their farms to be collectivised. From 1929, Stalin began to exterminate them as a class.

marxist a follower of the ideas of Karl Marx (1818–83). He believed that in a capitalist society, workers were exploited by the people they worked for. People were paid a wage to work to produce goods that were then sold at a higher price than they originally cost to make. The difference between the cost price and the price the object is sold at is called profit. Marx argued that the capitalists kept this profit. The workers could also be paid lower wages, as the lower the cost price, the bigger the profit made by the capitalists. For this reason, the capitalists and the workers would never see eye-to-eye, or have each other's best interests at heart. According to Marx, this situation created a class struggle. Marx said that eventually the workers would rebel against the capitalists and overthrow them. They would then establish a more equal society.

president the head of state of a republic.

proletariat the lower or working class, especially those living in industrial societies whose only possession (according to Marx) was the value of their work.

propaganda the deliberate and organised spread of information to make sure that people unquestioningly believe what you want them to believe. It is also used to refer to the information itself. Propaganda is not in itself good or bad. It depends on the purposes to which it is put and on who the audience are and what they believe.

republic a form of government where the people – or the people they elect – have power. Orwell's description of *Animal Farm* as a republic is clearly ironic (see Literary Terms) as the animals have no choice over Napoleon's decision to declare the farm to be one.

subversive someone or something that is working to overthrow a government.

totalitarian a government which has absolute control over as many aspects of its citizens' lives as possible. Most dictatorships are totalitarian.

tyrant a person who governs in an unjust and violent way. If they use their power in an unreasonable or selective way to oppress others, they can be said to be tyrannical.

TEST ANSWERS

TEST YOURSELF (Chapters 1–2)

A 1 Major *(Chapter 1)*
2 Snowball *(Chapter 2)*
3 Napoleon *(Chapter 2)*
4 Major *(Chapter 1)*
5 Boxer *(Chapter 1)*
6 Benjamin *(Chapter 1)*
7 Moses *(Chapter 2)*
8 Squealer *(Chapter 2)*

TEST YOURSELF (Chapters 3–4)

A 1 Snowball *(Chapter 4)*
2 Boxer *(Chapter 4)*
3 Squealer *(Chapter 3)*
4 The pigs *(Chapter 3)*
5 Boxer *(Chapter 3)*
6 The wild animals *(Chapter 3)*
7 Frederick and Pilkington *(Chapter 4)*

TEST YOURSELF (Chapters 5–6)

A 1 Squealer *(Chapter 5)*
2 Napoleon *(Chapter 6)*

3 Mollie *(Chapter 5)*
4 The crowd of animals
(Chapter 5)
5 The dogs *(Chapter 5)*

TEST YOURSELF (Chapters 7–9)

A 1 Boxer *(Chapter 7)*
2 Benjamin *(Chapter 9)*
3 Napoleon *(Chapter 7)*
4 One of the sheep *(Chapter 7)*
5 Frederick *(Chapter 8)*
6 Squealer *(Chapter 8)*
7 Benjamin *(Chapter 8)*

TEST YOURSELF (Chapter 10)

A 1 Clover *(Chapter 10)*
2 The sheep *(Chapter 10)*
3 Napoleon *(Chapter 10)*
4 The pigs and the dogs
(Chapter 10)
5 Napoleon *(Chapter 10)*
6 Pilkington *(Chapter 10)*

NOTES

Notes

GCSE and equivalent levels (£3.50 each)

Harold Brighouse
Hobson's Choice

Charles Dickens
Great Expectations

Charles Dickens
Hard Times

George Eliot
Silas Marner

William Golding
Lord of the Flies

Thomas Hardy
The Mayor of Casterbridge

Susan Hill
I'm the King of the Castle

Barry Hines
A Kestrel for a Knave

Harper Lee
To Kill a Mockingbird

Arthur Miller
A View from the Bridge

Arthur Miller
The Crucible

George Orwell
Animal Farm

J.B. Priestley
An Inspector Calls

J.D. Salinger
The Catcher in the Rye

William Shakespeare
Macbeth

William Shakespeare
The Merchant of Venice

William Shakespeare
Romeo and Juliet

William Shakespeare
Twelfth Night

George Bernard Shaw
Pygmalion

John Steinbeck
Of Mice and Men

Mildred D. Taylor
Roll of Thunder, Hear My Cry

James Watson
Talking in Whispers

A Choice of Poets

Nineteenth Century Short Stories

Poetry of the First World War

Advanced level (£3.99 each)

Margaret Atwood
The Handmaid's Tale

Jane Austen
Emma

Jane Austen
Pride and Prejudice

William Blake
Poems/Songs of Innocence and Songs of Experience

Emily Brontë
Wuthering Heights

Geoffrey Chaucer
Wife of Bath's Prologue and Tale

Joseph Conrad
Heart of Darkness

Charles Dickens
Great Expectations

F. Scott Fitzgerald
The Great Gatsby

Thomas Hardy
Tess of the D'Urbervilles

Seamus Heaney
Selected Poems

James Joyce
Dubliners

William Shakespeare
Antony and Cleopatra

William Shakespeare
Hamlet

William Shakespeare
King Lear

William Shakespeare
Macbeth

William Shakespeare
Othello

Mary Shelley
Frankenstein

Alice Walker
The Color Purple

John Webster
The Duchess of Malfi

Chinua Achebe
Things Fall Apart

Edward Albee
Who's Afraid of Virginia Woolf?

Jane Austen
Mansfield Park

Jane Austen
Northanger Abbey

Jane Austen
Persuasion

Jane Austen
Sense and Sensibility

Samuel Beckett
Waiting for Godot

John Betjeman
Selected Poems

Robert Bolt
A Man for All Seasons

Charlotte Brontë
Jane Eyre

Robert Burns
Selected Poems

Lord Byron
Selected Poems

Geoffrey Chaucer
The Franklin's Tale

Geoffrey Chaucer
The Knight's Tale

Geoffrey Chaucer
The Merchant's Tale

Geoffrey Chaucer
The Miller's Tale

Geoffrey Chaucer
The Nun's Priest's Tale

Geoffrey Chaucer
The Pardoner's Tale

Geoffrey Chaucer
Prologue to the Canterbury Tales

Samuel Taylor Coleridge
Selected Poems

Daniel Defoe
Moll Flanders

Daniel Defoe
Robinson Crusoe

Shelagh Delaney
A Taste of Honey

Charles Dickens
Bleak House

Charles Dickens
David Copperfield

Charles Dickens
Oliver Twist

Emily Dickinson
Selected Poems

John Donne
Selected Poems

Douglas Dunn
Selected Poems

George Eliot
Middlemarch

George Eliot
The Mill on the Floss

T.S. Eliot
The Waste Land

T.S. Eliot
Selected Poems

Henry Fielding
Joseph Andrews

E.M. Forster
Howards End

E.M. Forster
A Passage to India

John Fowles
The French Lieutenant's Woman

Elizabeth Gaskell
North and South

Oliver Goldsmith
She Stoops to Conquer

Graham Greene
Brighton Rock

Graham Greene
The Heart of the Matter

Graham Greene
The Power and the Glory

Thomas Hardy
Far from the Madding Crowd

Thomas Hardy
Jude the Obscure

Thomas Hardy
The Return of the Native

Thomas Hardy
Selected Poems

L.P. Hartley
The Go-Between

Nathaniel Hawthorne
The Scarlet Letter

Ernest Hemingway
A Farewell to Arms

Ernest Hemingway
The Old Man and the Sea

Homer
The Iliad

Homer
The Odyssey

Gerard Manley Hopkins
Selected Poems

Ted Hughes
Selected Poems

Aldous Huxley
Brave New World

Henry James
Portrait of a Lady

Ben Jonson
The Alchemist

Ben Jonson
Volpone

James Joyce
A Portrait of the Artist as a Young Man

John Keats
Selected Poems

Philip Larkin
Selected Poems

D.H. Lawrence
The Rainbow

D.H. Lawrence
Selected Stories

D.H. Lawrence
Sons and Lovers

D.H. Lawrence
Women in Love

Laurie Lee
Cider with Rosie

Christopher Marlowe
Doctor Faustus

Arthur Miller
Death of a Salesman

John Milton
Paradise Lost Bks I & II

John Milton
Paradise Lost IV & IX

Sean O'Casey
Juno and the Paycock

George Orwell
Nineteen Eighty-four

Y

John Osborne
Look Back in Anger

Wilfred Owen
Selected Poems

Harold Pinter
The Caretaker

Sylvia Plath
Selected Works

Alexander Pope
Selected Poems

Jean Rhys
Wide Sargasso Sea

William Shakespeare
As You Like It

William Shakespeare
Coriolanus

William Shakespeare
Henry IV Pt 1

William Shakespeare
Henry IV Pt II

William Shakespeare
Henry V

William Shakespeare
Julius Caesar

William Shakespeare
Measure for Measure

William Shakespeare
Much Ado About Nothing

William Shakespeare
A Midsummer Night's Dream

William Shakespeare
Richard II

William Shakespeare
Richard III

William Shakespeare
Sonnets

William Shakespeare
The Taming of the Shrew

William Shakespeare
The Tempest

William Shakespeare
The Winter's Tale

George Bernard Shaw
Arms and the Man

George Bernard Shaw
Saint Joan

Richard Brinsley Sheridan
The Rivals

R.C. Sherriff
Journey's End

Muriel Spark
The Prime of Miss Jean Brodie

John Steinbeck
The Grapes of Wrath

John Steinbeck
The Pearl

Tom Stoppard
Rosencrantz and Guildenstern are Dead

Jonathan Swift
Gulliver's Travels

John Millington Synge
The Playboy of the Western World

W.M. Thackeray
Vanity Fair

Mark Twain
Huckleberry Finn

Virgil
The Aeneid

Derek Walcott
Selected Poems

Oscar Wilde
The Importance of Being Earnest

Tennessee Williams
Cat on a Hot Tin Roof

Tennessee Williams
The Glass Menagerie

Tennessee Williams
A Streetcar Named Desire

Virginia Woolf
Mrs Dalloway

Virginia Woolf
To the Lighthouse

William Wordsworth
Selected Poems

W.B. Yeats
Selected Poems

York Notes – the Ultimate Literature Guides

York Notes are recognised as the best literature study guides.
If you have enjoyed using this book and have found it useful, you
can now order others directly from us – simply follow the ordering
instructions below.

HOW TO ORDER

Decide which title(s) you require and then order in one of the following ways:

Booksellers
All titles available from good bookstores.

By post
List the title(s) you require in the space provided overleaf,
select your method of payment, complete your name and
address details and return your completed order form and
payment to:

> *Addison Wesley Longman Ltd*
> *PO BOX 88*
> *Harlow*
> *Essex CM19 5SR*

By phone
Call our Customer Information Centre on 01279 623923 to
place your order, quoting mail number: HEYN1.

By fax
Complete the order form overleaf, ensuring you fill in your
name and address details and method of payment, and fax it
to us on 01279 414130.

By e-mail
E-mail your order to us on awlhe.orders@awl.co.uk listing
title(s) and quantity required and providing full name and
address details as requested overleaf. Please
quote mail number: HEYN1. Please do not
send credit card details by e-mail.

O

York Notes Order Form

Titles required:

Q   Price

Pr... ...ge without notice.
All...

Ple...
wo...
Longman Study Guides
(suitable for GCSE and A-level students)   🅛 Longman

Addison
Wesley
Longman

y